DARKNESS AT THE DAWNING

CRITICAL PERIODS OF HISTORY

Robert D. Cross and Paul K. Conkin, GENERAL EDITORS

American

THE ELECTION OF ANDREW JACKSON
by Robert V. Remini

RACE AND POLITICS *Bleeding Kansas and the Coming of the Civil War*
by James A. Rawley

LINCOLN AND THE FIRST SHOT
by Richard N. Current

IRISH-AMERICAN NATIONALISM, 1870-1890
by Thomas N. Brown

DARKNESS AT THE DAWNING *Race and Reform in the Progressive South*
by Jack Temple Kirby

McKINLEY, BRYAN AND THE PEOPLE
by Paul W. Glad

LABOR IN CRISIS *The Steel Strike of 1919*
by David Brody

TVA AND THE POWER FIGHT, 1933-1939
by Thomas K. McCraw

WAR AND SOCIETY *The United States, 1941-1945*
by Richard Polenberg

European

THE NAPOLEONIC REVOLUTION
by Robert B. Holtman

THE LONG FUSE *An Interpretation of the Origins of World War I*
by Laurence Lafore

WHY LENIN? WHY STALIN? *A Reappraisal of the Russian Revolution, 1900-1930*
by Theodore H. Von Laue

THE END OF GLORY *An Interpretation of the Origins of World War II*
by Laurence Lafore

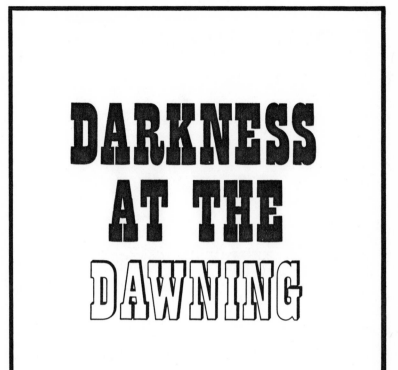

DARKNESS AT THE DAWNING

RACE AND REFORM
IN THE PROGRESSIVE SOUTH

Jack Temple Kirby

J. B. LIPPINCOTT COMPANY
Philadelphia New York Toronto

Paperbound: ISBN-0-397-47209-9
Clothbound: ISBN-0-397-47263-3
Library of Congress Catalog Card
Number: 77-161416
Printed in the United States of America
Interior design by Robert C. Digges
Cover design by Michael Louridas

99969

TO

Dorothy Simler Bulleit
(1910-1969)
and to her daughter
Ann Lorraine

CONTENTS

PROLOGUE

THE years between 1890 and World War I were critical and transitional for the American South. In this period, the great racial and political troubles resulting from the Civil War and Reconstruction were more or less concluded. Whites at last found peace and security of sorts in the elimination of black voters and the formal segregation of the races. Turning from this racial settlement, which they regarded as a great reform, they sought to improve their institutions and achieve "progress" on a wide front. Thus, the South joined what was called the "Progressive Movement." By World War I, a southern-born president and southern congressmen had led the nation into advanced reforms in a variety of areas. The southern states, too, moved toward the realization of the modern public service state.

This book is about the variegated and convoluted reform phenomenon known as "progressivism." Southern reform's scope was broad; change was rich and multidirectional. Reformers sought many goals desired elsewhere in the United States and frequently joined in national movements for better government, improved economic opportunity, and sundry "moral" reforms. However, in several senses, southern reform was different: the race issue was intimately involved with southern movements; and, fundamentally, the desire for

1

reform ran deeper and broader in the South than in other regions.

This was so simply because there was so much more to do in the impoverished South. Education was important everywhere, but a system of public schools barely existed in the South and had to be built from log cabin and paper foundations. The South's monopoly on the boll weevil and sharecropperism and its dire rural poverty—far worse than in the West—also prompted reforms peculiar to the South. Add to these reform movements the campaigns to abolish the peculiarly southern convict-lease system; other kinds of penal reform; the first practical applications of the commission and manager forms of city government; flourishing "sociology" movements for the study and correction of all manner of social ills; the statewide prohibition crusades of the period; the invention of the direct primary; and a vigorous anti-child-labor movement, and one begins to comprehend the breadth and complexity of reformism below the Potomac.[1]

The term "progressive" defies clear definition and should by all rights be banished from the lexicon of politics and philosophy. The word's singularity—as well as the singular "Progressive Movement"—is most misleading, for virtually every reformer in this and in subsequent ages has thought of himself as a "progressive." However, reforms as well as reformers are plural in goals and styles. Frequently "progressives" bitterly opposed each other. Some reformers, coming from fading elites, sought to reassert the influence of their class, along with an older value system. Downtrodden farmers and beleaguered small businessmen hoped to decentralize the economy and restore democracy; they often celebrated an idyllic Jeffersonian America as their model for a reformed society. Yet, other people who called themselves "progressives" belonged to the new breed of professionals, corporate organizers and efficiency experts who wished to rationalize and centralize the economy and government. Having little patience with the past, they looked to a brave future of technocracy and efficiency.

We can impose a superficial order upon progressivism by declaring it dichotomous.[2] On the one hand, there was the rural-based anti-trust tradition. This side of progressivism broadly represented the decentralizing, democratic, agrarian and localist interests of provincial America—especially the South and West. William Jennings Bryan, Josephus Daniels, and a raft of leaders of southern groups exemplified this tradition. On the other side of the dichotomy of progressivism was the urban-based, professional-minded, bureaucratizing and centralizing mode of thought. This style represented the futurists who triumphed in the Wilson administration and in the new "public service" state governments during the late 1910s and the 1920s. They included Theodore Roosevelt, who sought with big business to rationalize and protect an economy of giants—rather than slay the Wall Street behemoths, as would Bryan. Southerners such as John M. Parker of Louisiana, Alexander J. McKelway of North Carolina, and Westmoreland Davis of Virginia were also comfortable in the company of corporate systematizers and federal power; in their ways, they sought to apply business efficiency and centralized power to their pet reforms.

Yet, these descriptive cubby holes—the rural, traditional, antimonopoly "progressives" versus the urban, professional, business "progressives"—are accurate only in a very limited sense. Indeed—as we shall see particularly in Chapters II, III, and VII— there were so many separate styles of reform within each category and so much overlapping of goals and efforts that efforts to label reformers consistently become confusing and meaningless. "Progressivism," then, should be included with other enduring historical tags, such as the Enlightenment and the Romantic Movement, which cannot withstand rigorous definition. Progressivism encompassed far too many complexities and opposites; nevertheless the label will endure. However, only when "progressivism" is viewed as a device for self-identity, shared by the generation before the Great War, will it persist without confusion and endless, unproductive debate over semantics. At the turn of the century, a wide variety of Americans determined that they could come to grips decisively with all the evils left over from the nineteenth century; quite logically, they dubbed this pervasive mood of optimism and mastery "progressive." Since then, historians have adopted the label and sought in vain a simplified definition and explanation.

This book is also about the interaction of the race issue with reform in the South. To be specific, it is my contention that the great race settlement of 1890-1910—black disfranchisement and segregation—was itself the seminal "progressive" reform of the era. So far as most whites were concerned, counting out Negroes politically and socially made possible nearly every other reform they might undertake—from building better schools to closing the saloons. Some southern white reformers operated beyond the pale of racial politics. But an obsession with color drove many others into reform work. I shall pursue this theme later, in portraits of several remarkable men and their reforms.

Throughout, I use the terms "Negro" and "black" interchangeably in the fashion now common in the United States. The terms refer to all Americans with black African ancestors, taking into account no distinctions between those of mixed and pure racial descent. This arbitrary custom illustrates both the weakness of the expression "race" in the American vernacular and the whites' practice of exclusionism as a means of maintaining their own racial "purity." "Negro" and "race," then, should be recognized as symbols and inarticulate shibboleths representing white tribal belief and identity as much as they represent real, distinguishable beings and human categories. From the time of the earliest Virginia settlements well into the twentieth century, some whites elaborated their racial ideologies with care. Many of the white reformers of the progressive era discussed here were articulate men on questions of color. But the great mass of people have never expressed an elaborate, consistent concept of race.

Nonetheless, both the literate and the inarticulate probably shared some basic racial premises and goals over the generations: whites must subdue and subordinate nonwhites; this would express God's will, for He had put Africans on the earth in a place below that of whites. Whites further agreed that nonwhites were intellectually and biologically inferior to them. However, the real basis of the ideology of white supremacy was moral: blacks were innately inferior *morally*. This meant, simply, that nonwhites lacked a super ego, a set of built-in restraints, guilt, or other curbs on the libido. This association between color and morality makes understandable the centuries-long preoccupation of whites with alleged sexual aggression on the part of Negro males, with miscegenation generally, and with various institutions and reforms which might provide adequate curbs on the African libido.[3] Some "progressive" reforms were specifically tailored for this last purpose.

Finally, unless obvious in context, "reform" does not necessarily reflect a value judgment on my part. Rather, the word should be read much like the elusive word, "progressive." It has been a most flexible expression, used to describe almost any desired improvement in conditions. Since, for example, nearly all pre-World War I white Americans were racists—southerners most blatantly—"purifying the electorate" could logically be defined as eliminating nonwhite voters. Thus, reform, or doing the "right" thing as defined by progressives, might seem antireformist, even bizarre, in the 1970s. This is part of the fascination of reform in those times.

I

OUT OF THE DARK AGES

. . . consider what a train of blessings has followed upon the victories of 1898 and 1900. What magnificent progress industrially! How free have the moral forces found themselves, and with what power they have applied that freedom! . . . How the Commonwealth has leaped forward since the black bonds that bound her were cut asunder!

Since White Supremacy was established North Carolina is a new State.

JOSIAH WILLIAM BAILEY, 1912

The conscious unity of race [has become] . . . the broader ground of the new democracy.

EDGAR GARDNER MURPHY, 1904

IN the South, an era of reform called "progressive" by its contemporaries began with a new system of racial control. The craftily devised disfranchisement of blacks and poor whites and the achievement 'of legal segregation ended a quarter century of uncertainty and white controversy over the

place of nonwhites. This great race settlement laid the foundation for most other reforms during the era. Some whites
opposed the settlement; literate, middle class people profited
most and became the most articulate reformers. No one class
held a monopoly on initiating and executing the settlement;
it was essentially the work of a white consensus. From Mississippi in 1890 to Virginia in 1902 and to Oklahoma in
1907—the disfranchisers and segregators spoke of reform and
of entering a new period of moral and material progress. To
them, a generation of chaos had ended. The South left its
dark ages, its long unhappy season of troubles.

The Civil War and Reconstruction destroyed a two centuries old system of social control and labor supply, lowered
land values, and left a critical shortage of farm credit. Landless and muleless blacks and whites sought places while
landholders sought fieldhands without wages to give them or
credit to offer them. Finally, country merchants—themselves
deeply indebted to inventory suppliers—bound land and labor
together with the crop lien arrangement. Cotton prices were
high enough in the late 1860s to warrant the risk of advancing seed, plows, food, clothing and other necessities to share-
croppers during the growing season—all against the expected
crop. The merchants midwifed a reborn cotton kingdom.
Production advanced to new records, but prices began a long
downward slide: from 29¢ per pound in 1868 to about 11¢
in 1890, to 7½¢ in 1892, to a pathetic 4.9¢ in 1898. It cost
7¢ per pound to grow cotton.

Scarce credit and low prices swept farmers into ruin and
despair. The costs for fertilizers, jute bagging, and railway
shipments remained high. Many croppers, hopelessly indebted to supply merchants, fled in the night to seek new
places and fresh liens. Merchants raised prices and lien costs
to recoup losses. They insisted that cotton, which always
brought cash, be planted to the virtual exclusion of other
crops—and these crops might have saved the soil. The same
rules prevailed in the tobacco country. Such was the self-
destructive economic impasse that afflicted Jefferson's
"chosen people of God" and that created the class and racial

struggle that stormed throughout the last quarter of the century.[1]

Agricultural distress invited political agitation. From the 1870s through the 1890s—Grangers, independent Democrats, Greenbackers, the Virginia Readjusters, Farmers' Alliance-men and, finally, the Populists proposed a variety of reforms. They demanded state commissions to regulate railroad and other business corporations, improved educational opportunities and agricultural information services, democratizing political reforms, and protective legislation for allied urban laborers. Alliance-Populists directly attacked the central problem of credit—first with cooperatively owned warehouses, exchanges, and gins, later with appeals for federally subsidized storage and credit facilities. Often flamboyant, romantic—even paranoid—the rural reformers nevertheless came to grips with their dilemma and, while ultimately defeated, they won significant victories and set ideological precedents.

The rural revolt also revived the stresses of Reconstruction. Within the state Democratic parties, white men divided along economic and social lines and bid against each other for the black vote. When blacks chose factions, they realistically sided with the white group which offered them office, protection, and the continued exercise of their civil rights. The planter-business—or conservative—faction usually bid higher. Outnumbered planters, large farmers, businessmen and townspeople sorely needed the voting help they gained by "fusions" with blacks. Sometimes conservatives also assumed the old paternal pose of protecting the "helpless darkies" against "nigger-baiting white trash." These planter-business patrons stood for government by the "best people," based upon sound economic principles and minimal governmental services. Such principles—along with a low tax base—helped them to rationalize the paucity of public schools, the infamous convict-leasing system, and inadequate informational services for farmers. Poorer white farmers leaped to the conclusion that black men blocked the pathway to their every goal.

In several areas—notably North Carolina and northern

Georgia—white and black farmers temporarily but warily co-
operated in overturning established Democratic regimes.
Georgia's Tom Watson made such eloquent appeals to economic common sense that both whites and blacks set aside
their fears and forged an interracial Populist alliance. However, well-founded mutual suspicions made these extraordinary fusions shaky and tentative at best. More frequently,
white Democrats of all social classes accomplished by force
the *de facto* disfranchisement of Negroes by the end of the
1880s or in the early 1890s; they then formalized the fait
accompli by constitutional revision. Mississippi led the way

From the mid-1870s through the 1880s, black Republicans,
white Republicans, regular (conservative) Democrats, and
various insurgent groups representing rural whites all contended for offices in Mississippi. In the heavily black river
counties, black Republicans and white conservative Democrats often joined together to form successful local, congressional, and statewide tickets. White Republicans, white
independents, Greenbackers, and others jockeyed and bar-
gained for power—sometimes in tandem, sometimes separately. Bitterness and violence grew in each succeeding contest for the black vote. Insurgent farmers particularly re-
sented the black-conservative alliance and terrorized blacks
to keep them away from polls. The crisis drew to a climax
in 1889–1890. As Republicans took control of both houses of
the U.S. Congress, Mississippi's Negroes and other southern
blacks rejoiced in the new prospects for patronage and for a
reassertion of federal protection of civil rights. Young Representative Henry Cabot Lodge of Massachusetts introduced
his famous "force bill" which, if passed, would have provided
for federal supervision of congressional elections.

Frightened whites now acted with new boldness. Frank
Burkitt, president of the Mississippi Farmers' Alliance and
an avowed champion of poorer whites, demanded a state
constitutional convention to eliminate blacks from politics.
U.S. Senator Edward Cary Walthall—Delta aristocrat, corporation lawyer, and a fusion man—opposed disfranchisement.

Into this standoff stepped the other senator, General J. Z. George, a political wizzard who had managed to combine a lucrative corporate legal practice with a vast popularity among back country farmers. George sided with the would-be disfranchisers and assumed leadership of the convention movement.

Support for the disfranchisement proposal involved more than mere political expedience or racial phobias. Rural prohibitionists, for example, were indignant that all thirty-five of the remaining wet counties in Mississippi were heavily black and were mainly in the fusion-principle Delta. Prohibitionists deduced that diabolical liquor interests were in league with immoral black politicians. Furthermore, Farmers' Alliancemen despaired of the improvement of agricultural conditions or such reforms as state regulation of railroads and insurance companies as long as conservatives controlled black votes. Frank Burkitt's analysis reflected the anger of the poorer whites across the state: The opponent's of disenfranchisement were "a class of corrupt office-seekers" plotting to capitalize upon "the immense political power conferred upon the negro counties." They "hypocritically raised the howl of white supremacy while they debauched the ballot boxes." By such "infamous means [they] made themselves potent factors in [the] State and county governments, and . . . under the pretense of maintaining a rule of intelligence . . . disregarded the rights of the blacks," wasted public money, raised taxes, "plunged the State into debt, and actually dominated the will of the white people through the instrumentality of the stolen negro vote."

Many Delta conservatives also had ample reasons to reform the vote. Elders mourned that the younger generation was fast learning the sordid political tactics that had been used since Reconstruction days: ballot box stuffing, "bull dozing"— intimidation of—voters, murder, and mob violence. A former Confederate colonel solemnly observed: "The old men of the present generation can't afford to die and leave their children with shot guns in their hands, a lie in their mouths and perjury on their souls, in order to defeat the negroes. The constitution can be made so this will not be necessary." Another conservative frankly admitted that there had "not been a full vote and a fair count in Mississippi since 1875" and that they had been "preserving the ascendancy of the white people by revolutionary methods." Thus, "thoughtful men everywhere foresaw that there was disaster somewhere along the line of such a policy as certainly as there is a righteous judgment for nations as well as men. No man can be in favor of perpetuating the election methods which have prevailed . . . since 1875 who is not a moral idiot." If good government, fair political practices, peace, and public morality were ever to return to Mississippi, then decisive reform was imperative. Thus many of the river country aristocrats joined the back country farmers for good reasons of their own and made black disfranchisement a goal of all white classes. Proponents frequently referred to the proposed electoral reform as "progressive" and characterized enemies as reactionary standpatters or mindless opponents of progress.

In August 1890, the convention met in Jackson. After considerable disagreement over means, delegates decided to limit the suffrage by a poll tax, long residency requirement, and a literacy test. Chief among the convention's problems was assuring poor whites that they would not lose the ballot along with blacks. This assurance took the form of the "understanding clause," which gave white Democratic registrars wide discretion in reading aloud sections of the law and judging applicants' ability to explain or "understand" it. In no place did the constitutional amendments mention race. The United States Supreme Court would accept this formula, the famous Mississippi Plan, eight years later in *Williams v. Mississippi.*

Implementation of the Mississippi Plan marked only a symbolic end—a *de jure* conclusion—to the long battle over blacks in politics. Accelerated violence and intimidation in the late 1880s had already disqualified most Negro voters in Mississippi, but white reformers insisted upon the added security of constitutional change. Only with this security, would whites feel completely free to divide against each other in pursuit of varied economic and social interests. However, following the demise of the black voter, regular Democrats would consistently turn the weapon of franchise restriction against the radical, or potentially radical, poor white. Some Farmers' Alliancemen, Populists, and Republicans predicted this betrayal. Nevertheless, in those hysterical days, the bitterest white class conflict gave way before the solvent of race loyalty. Some cynical regular Democrats hastened the white fusion by advocating rural causes such as currency inflation and the regulation of big business. The fragile white consensus did not survive long. Yet, the intraracial moratorium on conflict endured long enough to count out the Negroes, first by force and then by law.

Most white Republicans of both North and South virtually abandoned blacks and, by the late 1880s, made "lily whiteism" their national policy. Southern Republicans vied with Democrats in their negrophobia. In 1888, for example, the Republican gubernatorial candidate in North Carolina charged in a public address that Democratic President Grover Cleveland had dined at the White House with former abolitionist Frederick Douglass and his white wife and that on another occasion he had "kissed a negro wench." A Democratic county chairman desperately sought an "authoratative [sic] denial of these dirty charges."

During the next dozen years, the genius of the Mississippi formula and the permissive apathy of most Yankees prepared the way for black disfranchisement in one southern state after another. The fateful step was delayed here and there as white political factions continued the contest for black alliances or hesitated—before the *Williams* decision—for fear of federal court intervention. However, variations of the Mississippi theme played again and again.

South Carolina, with its black majority and bitter intrastate sectional hatreds, was next. After assuming leadership of the Farmers' Alliance, upcountry demagogue Benjamin R.

"Pitchfork Ben" Tillman seized power in the Democratic party and, in 1890, swept aside the conservative forces of General Wade Hampton. As governor, Tillman established virtually undisputed control over state politics. His followers controlled or quashed through intimidation remaining pockets of black voting strength, finishing a job begun years before. It was only a matter of time before a constitutional convention gave legal dignity to "white man's rule." A cheering crowd of white militants in Tillman's home county put the charge bluntly: "We have got the negro down, and by God, we are going to keep him down."

A few low country conservative fusionists and extraordinary blacks such as Robert Smalls and William Whipper, protested the disfranchisement movement. But Tillman easily secured the support of most of the prestigious conservatives well before the convention of 1895. Tillman himself generaled the affair, but his forces had invaluable assistance from Hamptonite lawyers, such as the Charlestonian John P. K. Bryan. Like Mississippi's, the new suffrage provisions included long residence requirements, the poll tax, and "discreet" election boards which could apply "understanding" and "reading and writing tests." The new constitution also established prohibition, another Tillmanite reform.

Three years later, Louisiana whites contributed the grandfather clause to the disfranchisement lexicon. The clause permitted illiterate whites whose grandfathers had voted to remain qualified, while other measures eliminated illiterate blacks—the grandsons of slaves—from voting lists. In the following year (1899), North Carolina whites adopted this innovation. Here, regular Democrats had just broken the back of a state government dominated by a Populist-Republican fusion which included many blacks. After a racial reign of terror in the port city of Wilmington and the escalated intimidation of blacks throughout the state, Democrats prepared to secure order, their own ascendancy, and "white man's government." The brightest young reform leaders, Josephus Daniels and Charles B. Aycock, were among the vanguard of the disfranchisement movement. Daniels, editor of the militantly anti-Negro Raleigh *News and Observer*, had traveled to Louisiana in order personally to study the grandfather clause. He and Aycock forcefully maintained that electoral reform would lead directly to better schools and roads and to the regulation of big business—but first had to come white unity. They accomplished disfranchisement by a constitutional amendment in 1900. Simultaneously, Aycock became governor and began a fruitful reform era in North Carolina.

Constitutional revision came to Alabama in 1901. There, in their struggle to diminish the Populist and insurgent Democratic electorates, planter and business interests adopted the disfranchisement issue. Hill country whites bitterly and unsuccessfully fought voter restriction. But reformers among the regular Democrats, such as Braxton Bragg Comer, supported the new constitutional provisions and later welded a reform coalition of businessmen and farmers within the new political order.

The heyday of white class conflict and the contest for the black vote came early in Virginia. Under the Readjuster party label, an anticonservative coalition of black and white farmers, laborers, and opportunists captured the legislature and governorship in 1879 and 1881. Readjuster leaders such as William Mahone and H. H. Riddleberger responded to farmer-labor demands, but a conservative counterattack mounted early. Mahone's ruthless political tactics, the biracial strength of the party, and its labor support—compounded by an unfortunate race riot in Danville in 1883—galvanized enough frightened Democrats to turn out the Readjusters. In 1883 younger leaders remodeled and strengthened the Democratic party and, two years later, Democrat Fitzhugh Lee was elected governor. The new-model party organization, headed by corporation attorney Thomas S. Martin, continued to buy and manipulate black votes, but the 1894 Walton Election Law, which discriminated against both black and white illiterates, catalyzed the withdrawal of blacks from politics.

At the end of the century, however, the conservative, corporate orientation of the Martin Democratic organization generated an intraparty revolt. Respectable, middle-class young men—such as Carter Glass, Andrew Jackson Montague, and Allan Caperton Braxton led the insurgency. These self-styled progressives were motivated by a combination of political opportunism and a nostalgic, idealistic desire to return Virginia to the elan, morality, and public order which, they thought, prevailed in antebellum times. In this vein, they called for the demise of "ring influence" and corporate dominance in government and for a constitutional convention to formalize electoral reform (disfranchisement) and to establish a regulatory corporation commission. Montague was elected governor and, in a grand convention (1901–1902), Glass and Braxton won the electoral and economic reforms they sought. Thus, Virginia immediately adopted the literacy test, poll tax, and modern corporation commission. The progressive reformers represented a different generation and a somewhat different class from the white Mississippi consensus of a dozen years before but, significantly, they also coupled racial settlement with other reforms.

White Georgia accomplished black disfranchisement in a series of legal steps, beginning in the 1890s. In 1908, under the urging of Atlanta progressive Hoke Smith and redneck messiah Tom Watson, the state finally adopted the literacy test and grandfather clause. States with relatively few blacks used only the poll tax and random intimidation to insure the new order; this occurred in Florida (1889), Tennessee (1890), Arkansas (1893), and Texas (1902). Oklahoma, a new state with a large southern immigrant population, entered the union in 1907 with a "radical" constitution concocted by social reformer Kate Barnard, by William Jennings Bryan, and by a coalition of labor union representatives and farmers. The Sooner State's law combined such innovative devices as the direct primary, initiative and referendum provisions, and a strong corporation commission with suffrage restriction via the poll tax and literacy test. Thus, the official work of undoing Reconstruction was concluded in the midst of the twentieth century's first reform movement.

As southern whites removed blacks from politics they took parallel legislative steps to eliminate interracial propinquity, to insure the separation of the two races by law. Discrimination and white-imposed separation were hardly new phenomena—nor were they even peculiarly southern. A national rehearsal of more than a century preceded the movement. Race slavery, supported by an elaborate ideology of African inferiority, was well developed in English America by the end of the seventeenth century. In the late eighteenth century the ideal of natural rights, the tumult of war, and favorable economic conditions promoted emancipation north of Delaware and excluded slavery in the Northwest Territory. Individual southerners manumited thousands of bondsmen in the old seaboard South. Nevertheless, the abolition of slavery did not mean an equitable racial adjustment anywhere. A pattern of separation developed in the North as early as the 1790s. In Philadelphia and elsewhere Negroes seceded from incompatible white Methodist and Baptist congregations and formed their own churches. White mechanics and laborers excluded free blacks from their guilds and unions. Segregation, both customary and legal, came to pervade transportation, public accommodations, education—even burial grounds. During the Jacksonian period the rising white "common man" helped disfranchise blacks in several northeastern states. There was no nonwhite suffrage west of Pennsylvania and north of the Ohio until 1870. Some Yankees were bitter—as southern whites would be half a century later—that black voters generally sided with the "aristocrats"—in this case, the Federalists and the Whigs. Disfranchisement (or exclusion from the moment of statehood) was a practical device for reducing the opposition electorate and a symbol of white determination to assert black inferiority.[2]

In the antebellum southern countryside, where the vast majority of colored peoples lived, the institution of slavery and its requisite close supervision precluded the northern

pattern of segregation. However, southern cities forecast the
future; there, significant numbers of free Negroes and hired-
out slaves worked at skilled and unskilled jobs on the streets,
wharves, and in shops, factories and white homes. Freeman
and slave mingled, taking care of themselves in largely segregated shanty towns on the outskirts of the cities. Whites
gradually became alarmed at the insufficiency of caste distinctions and the inadequate supervision of urban blacks. The
Denmark Vesey conspiracy in Charleston (1822) and subsequent rumored plots convinced many whites that slavery was
dangerous in the city. Whites caused urban slavery to decline in the latter part of the antebellum period. Meanwhile,
city whites pioneered in both customary and *de jure* discrimination and segregation. New Orleans laws enforced
racial separation in public accommodations as early as 1816.
Blacks were not allowed in public parks there or in Charleston, Savannah, and Baltimore. *De facto* segregation in jails,
hospitals, theatres, and cemeteries was common.

Broadened customary segregation followed slavery's violent
death during the war. Whites and blacks in many areas
simultaneously withdrew from the old intimacies, duties, and
obligations imposed by the peculiar institution of slavery.
Some of the freedmen moved into all-black enclaves or left
the South altogether. Some whites believed that no racial
adjustment short of reenslavement was possible. Others
thought that the separatist race "instinct" made segregation
inevitable and a minimal requirement for racial peace. Only
one thing was certain: at no time previously in the American
experience had blacks been accorded real equality, except in
a very local or restricted context. Now, in the postwar years,
southern blacks and whites repeated in their own environment many northern precedents. Southern freedmen withdrew from white-dominated churches throughout the region.
Cultural differences and the experience of enslavement had
produced different spiritual needs and demanded separate
Afro-American religions. Also, black ministers—many of them
Baptist and Methodist missionaries from the North—had a

self-interest in building their own churches. The result was a full-blown pattern of southern church segregation even during Reconstruction. Southern history also repeated the northern model in public education, although blacks fared better, perhaps, in the South during Reconstruction than they had in the antebellum North. White northerners generally excluded Negroes from the very schools they were taxed to help support. For the first time, Reconstruction regimes introduced broad—however inferior—public education for both races. With few exceptions—notably the New Orleans system—the schools were racially segregated. Most whites, natives and "carpetbaggers" demanded separation and threatened to withdraw their children and destroy the systems if radical reformers sought to impose school integration. In South Carolina, whites and a number of blacks contended that racial co-education would "aggravate and extend the 'war of the races' to the children." School segregation, then, was the first massive official accommodation to racial antipathies in the postbellum South.

Meanwhile, the Mississippi legislature passed the first postwar Jim Crow law in November 1865, before the radical phase of Reconstruction began. This legislation prohibited "any negro, freedman, or mullato" from riding in first class cars on railroads—although whites continued to ride in second class cars with nonwhites. Republicans repealed the law five years later but, despite this and other legislation providing free access to public accommodations, the color line usually prevailed. In 1874, Congressman John R. Lynch "retired without protest" when asked to leave a white table in the Holly Springs railroad dining room. Such examples of segregation and discrimination, laws to the contrary notwithstanding, are to be found in every southern state between the end of the war and 1890. Nevertheless, just as many examples of physical integration and white acceptance, sufferance, or indifference are readily available. The only rule of race relations and racial ideology in these years was inconsistency— or chaos, as many insecure whites thought of it.

White southerners divided widely on race policy, with numberless nuances within each broad category of opinion. The poorer whites appear to have been the most militant negrophobes. Closest to the black masses in economic status, the poor usually had the most to fear from the spector of "equality." Thus, it was often they who made physical war on blacks and demanded clearcut, legislated race distinctions. Poorer whites had been the rank and file, if not the leaders, of Reconstruction Ku Klux Klans and other terrorist groups, and it was the spokesmen of this class who pushed the first post-Reconstruction Jim Crow laws in the late 1880s. Economically and socially secure whites, many of them former slaveholders, often took a conciliatory and paternal stand. They seldom felt the compelling personal need to underline their "superiority" with a rigid color line. Thus, some members of the white elite, such as Wade Hampton, actively stood in the way of segregation. Most, however, were passive before redneck fury and gave way when confronted. Sometimes, for reasons of political expediency if not actual conviction, planters and businessmen led the segregators and disfranchisers; such was at least partly the case in Mississippi, Alabama, North Carolina, and Virginia.

A handful of southern whites held beliefs bordering on egalitarianism. In 1884, George Washington Cable of New Orleans, foremost novelist of the Lower South, confirmed gentleman, and a twice-wounded Confederate veteran, penned "The Freedman's Case in Equity," an extraordinary article published in *Century Magazine*. Cable indicted fellow southern whites for their race hatred, segregationist sentiments, discrimination, and their cruel exploitation of blacks in the convict-leasing system. Cable nonetheless insisted that such racist extremism was not actually representative of the white South. There was, he held, a vast, disapproving "silent South." He hoped to scold this silent majority into countervailing action in behalf of blacks: "But is not silent endurance criminal?" he asked. "Speech may be silvern and silence golden; but if a lump of gold is only big enough, it can drag us to the bottom of the sea and hold us there while all the world sails over us."

Cable's nobility of sentiment won for him enduring infamy and immediate reprobation throughout the South. Among the bitter published retorts was that of Charles Gayarré, Louisiana planter-lawyer, Creole historian, and erstwhile friendly acquaintance of Cable. Writing in the New Orleans *Times-Democrat*, eighty-year-old Gayarré termed Cable's *Century* article libelous and impertinent and decried the novelist's "wish to bring together, by every possible means, the blacks and whites in the most familiar and closest friction everywhere, in every imaginable place of resort, save the private parlor and the private bed chamber, into which, for the present, a disagreeable intrusion may not be permitted." Old paternalist Gayarré vied with the poorest whites in his segregationist ardor, and admirers dubbed him "Champion of the South." Henry W. Grady, publisher of the Atlanta *Constitution* and the paladin of southern industry, joined Gayarré in a withering rebuke to Cable. Such attacks influenced Cable to move north, but he was not the last to dramatize white differences of feeling.

Lewis Harvie Blair and Thomas E. Watson, two men wholly unlike one another, opposed racial extremism on economic grounds. An elderly Confederate veteran, Blair was a prosperous Richmond businessman of good family and a compulsive curmudgeon. Posing as hard realist and materialist, Blair in 1889 debunked the recently fabricated myth of an industrial "new" South, statistically exposed the section's poverty, and concluded that prosperity was impossible until six million blacks were educated, granted real equality, and accepted as valuable members of the political economy. Farmer-lawyer Tom Watson, of Thomson, Georgia, came to roughly the same conclusion via the route of third-party politics and the farmers' struggle against conservative Democrats. He argued: unite blacks and whites whose economic interests correspond; be certain that they understand their self-interests, and color antagonisms will abate as they achieve their political and

economic goals. As a Populist congressman he appealed
directly to black voters, in Georgia and throughout the South,
until Democrats gerrymandered and defrauded him out of his
seat in the early 1890s. Watson later became a violent race-
baiter himself, but his earlier radicalism highlights this age
of controversy.

South Carolina's Republicans wrote a strong civil rights
law during Reconstruction which, along with Wade Hampton's post-1877 politics of fusion and accommodation, helped
partly to blur the color line. Customary segregation apparently prevailed in small country towns throughout the state,
and the better hotels in the cities were generally for whites
only. Yet, Charleston and Columbia blacks regularly attended
concerts, circuses, bars, ice cream parlors, and restaurants
with whites, even though they frequently had to accept segregated seating arrangements inside.

In 1875, a black waiter from North Carolina announced his
intention to travel by rail from Raleigh to Savannah in order
to test the federal Civil Rights Act of that year. The *Raleigh
Sentinel* later reported that the first class ride was an un-
segregated success from the point of view of the testor. The
celebrated experience of T. McCants Stewart came fully a
decade later—two years after the Supreme Court's reversal of
the Civil Rights Act and eight years after the fall of the last
Reconstruction state regime. Stewart, a black journalist on a
mission for the *New York Age*, journeyed through Virginia,
North Carolina, and his native South Carolina. Turning southward from the nation's capital, he recorded: "I put a chip on
my shoulder, and inwardly dared any man to knock it off."
Apparently no one did. Stewart discovered that whites rode
next to him on the train without notice, much less protest.
In Petersburg, Virginia, heart of the Old Dominion's black
belt, he was courteously served in an integrated dining room
where "the whites at the [same] table appeared not to note
my presence." Whites and blacks dined together frequently
at the same tables in both Carolinas. Stewart concluded
ecstatically: "I can ride in first class cars on the railroads

and in the streets. I can go into saloons and get refreshments even as in New York. I can stop in and drink a glass of soda and be more politely waited upon than in some parts of New England." Indeed, he exclaimed: "the Palmetto State leads the South in some things. May she go on advancing in liberal practices and prospering throughout her borders; and may she be like a leaven unto the South . . . leading this our blessed section on and on in the way of liberty, justice, equality, truth, and righteousness."

Like most other states, Virginia was a welter of unorthodoxy and inconsistency. Between the ending of slavery and the turn of the century no broadly accepted racial code is discernable. Black South Carolina Congressman James H. Rainey was thrown out of a Suffolk hotel in 1875, but McCants Stewart ate peacefully at the depot restaurant near Petersburg ten years later. As early as 1870, the Orange and Alexandria Railroad adopted the Jim Crow car; yet in the 1880s, Stewart and other blacks rode other lines without white reaction; observers noted that Negroes sat in first class cars everywhere in the state. Only in 1900 did white Virginia legislators get around to codifying Jim Crow on the railways—thereby imposing through the majesty of the law an orthodoxy that had not existed before.

This late-blooming *de jure* segregation movement, which reached the Upper South about the turn of the century, began in the Gulf states late in the 1880s. Along with the demand for electoral reform, legislators began to insist upon racial separation on the trains. Florida passed a Jim Crow railroad law in 1887; Mississippi, in 1888; neighboring Louisiana, in 1890; and Alabama, Arkansas, Kentucky and Georgia, in 1891. In 1895, Booker T. Washington announced in Atlanta his formal acceptance of segregation; whites hastened to crown him chief "spokesman for the Negro race" and accelerated the legal separation movement. Upper South states and localities elaborated and extended Jim Crow laws to include separation and exclusion in streetcars, taxis, hotels, and restaurants. The federal Supreme Court validated the principle of "separate and equal" in the famous *Plessy v. Ferguson* decision of 1896.

What the embattled rural representative began, city whites adopted and systematized. *De facto* residential segregation apparently developed in newer inland southern cities, but the old seaboard towns remained a patchwork of black and white neighborhoods. Here, *de facto* integration was a fact of life. Among these cities, Baltimore took the lead in legal separation in the fall of 1910. When a Negro moved into a white block, neighborhood whites demonstrated before the city council. It responded with an ordinance which forbade either whites or blacks from moving into blocks dominated by the opposite race. Inexperienced Baltimore segregators worked out certain technicalities which did not at first withstand scrutiny by the courts. Meanwhile, the urban movement spread south; Greenville, South Carolina and Atlanta soon copied the Baltimore style of neighborhood segregation.

In the spring of 1912, the Virginia General Assembly enacted the first statewide formula for urban segregation. Its guidelines invited city governments to draw racial maps and make them available to the public for refinement and correction. After six months, the maps became *prima facie* evidence of a city's racial boundaries; thereafter, anyone taking up residence in the district of another race was guilty of a misdemeanor punishable by law. Roanoke and Portsmouth took advantage of the state legislation; Richmond and Norfolk passed somewhat different ordinances of their own. In 1913, North Carolina considered but did not pass statewide legislation. Nonetheless, Winston-Salem copied Richmond's method of block designation by race and forbade anyone to move into a block where his race was not in the majority. Some Lower South cities implemented the even more complicated segregation code which was invented in Norfolk. This phase of the movement spread southward, then westward, to Charleston, Mobile, Meridian and beyond. The New Orleans council devised yet another code which required prospective residents of either race to secure the consent of a neighborhood majority before moving in. By the end of 1913, *de jure* segregation of cities had become a hot issue all the way to Oklahoma City, where whites dynamited the home of a black newcomer.

Only in the new century, then, did the South—from Maryland to the Southwest—consolidate a final racial settlement and a new orthodoxy. Some variances in whites' opinions and behavior would persist for a while, but the great inconsistencies of the 1870s, 1880s, and 1890s had virtually disappeared by 1906, when Middle Western journalist Ray Stannard Baker began his tour of the region, "following the color line." Shortly before, Professor W. E. B. DuBois of Atlanta University sadly observed that, in contrast to previous decades and despite continued workaday "physical contact and daily intermingling, there is almost no community of intellectual life or point of transference where the thoughts and feelings of one race can come into direct contact and sympathy with the thoughts and feelings of the other." Blacks and whites "go to separate churches," he wrote. "They live in separate sections, they are strictly separated in all public gatherings, they travel separately, and they are beginning to read different papers and books."

This, however, had been precisely the goal of the white reformers. Now white men of all classes were at least partly freed of their racial obsessions. Putting these aside, they could turn to other matters. This was the spirit of the new century. Jim Crow rescued the white South from the dark uncertainties of heterodoxy. Now, with order and orthodoxy, anything might be possible.

II

THE SOUTH VERSUS LEVIATHAN

*In these later years I have seen, with gratification,
that my work in the good old Populist days was not
in vain. The Progressive party has adopted our platform, clause by clause, plank by plank.*

MARY E. LEASE, 1914

THE most potent force for southern reform lay in the frustrations and yearnings of the rural and small town masses.
Among them, traditional agrarian pride lived on, wounded by
rural America's declining fortunes. Countrymen expressed
their outrage primarily against the economic institutions
which they believed had colonized them: the railroads, New
York banks, huge manufacturers—or generically, the "trusts."
The essential reform urge of the masses was antimonopo-
listic. They hoped that, if the big business leviathan could
only be subdued and economic democracy restored, the prestige and quality of provincial living would improve. The
campaigns for schools, better roads, more farmer services,
and the elimination of the saloon were closely associated
with the antitrust movement. However, the antimonopoly
spirit was predominant; it virtually unified southerners from
Virginia to Texas and provided the great connecting link be-

tween the rural protests of the nineteenth century and those of the twentieth.

Antitrust reformism had many styles. Along the seaboard especially (as we shall see later) it was a moderate—almost decorous—movement, led by the respectable middle class. In the Lower and Trans-Mississippi Souths, where conditions were most desperate, it was often quixotic, radical, and productive of frustration, racial diversions, and violence. Overall, the tone of rural protest in the early twentieth century was perhaps less rancorous than during the Populist days The ranks of the rednecks were decimated in some areas by the poll tax and the literacy test. Yet, in many respects, the basic format of the 1880s and 1890s persisted: antimonopoly crusading was marked by the rhetoric of class struggle, moral absolutism, provincial outrage, and race-baiting. The very persistence of nineteenth century ills, along with the endurance of certain aging rural mass leaders, encouraged this continuity.

South Carolina's Benjamin R. Tillman mellowed somewhat in the U.S. Senate, but his successor as governor, Cole Blease, vied with Georgia's Tom Watson and Alabama's J. Thomas Heflin in violent, preposterous language and demagogic posturing. Blease, purporting to be the champion of poor whites, was an utter fraud. He baited blacks, harrangued the upcountry "wool hat boys," and railed against the "aristocrats" and the "trusts;" in power, he covertly opposed most so-called progressive reforms. Blease's success in manipulating the voters through reform rhetoric demonstrates the persistence of the rural plight, poor education, business regulation, and child labor legislation as viable issues—as well as the credulousness of the white masses in the hands of a demagogue.[1]

Tom Watson, who did not hold office after his season with Populism until he went to the senate in 1918, nevertheless held the balance of power in Georgia from around 1900. By manipulating his loyal clay-hill followers, Svengali-like, Watson pursued one erratic madness after another during these years. In 1906, he backed Atlanta reformer Hoke Smith's successful gubernatorial bid, partly because Smith agreed to black disfranchisement. Then, two years later, he sided with Smith's enemies. For years, he exploited his influence with the masses, using his various newspapers to crusade against the Pope—a "fat old Dago"—Socialists, Wall Street, Jews, and the blacks. Between 1913 and 1915 he issued a deluge of incredible libel against Leo Frank, accused Jewish murderer of a young gentile girl, and Frank's defenders. Probably as a direct result of Watson's rabble rousing, a white mob attacked the executive mansion in Atlanta and drove the governor from the state. Meanwhile, a motorized gang abducted Frank from prison, drove him to another city, then lynched and unspeakably mutilated him.

To the west, popular leaders were as bizarre as Blease and Watson but more attentive to popular issues and somewhat more effective at antitrust and allied reforms. In 1903, following Mississippi's adoption of the direct primary system, James K. Vardaman won the governorship. Champion of the upcountry and an implacable enemy of the Delta aristocracy, railroads, and insurance companies, Vardaman—"The White Chief"—was adept at the image-making and showmanship required of a demagogue. He appeared at the hustings aboard a lumber wagon drawn by pale oxen, dressed in a white suit with flowing tails and wearing his hair in long waving locks. A florid racist, Vardaman promised to destroy the ragtail black school system of Mississippi, campaigned for repeal of the Fourteenth and Fifteenth Amendments, and smiled at lynching. However, he avidly sought free schools for whites, more effective corporate regulation, and credit relief for farmers. If Vardaman was not wholly successful in achieving his reform goals, the fault probably lay less with his efforts than in the intractability of his enemies and the depth of Mississippi's social and economic problems.

Vardaman's heir, rambunctious little Theodore G. "The Man" Bilbo, was no less a racial extremist but was a more successful governor. Elected in 1915, after a vindictive,

abusive campaign against his enemies, Bilbo pressed through
a remarkable brace of reforms which finally brought Mississippi into the twentieth century. His new tax commission
equalized taxation in the state, raising rates most notably in
fourteen Delta counties. His achievements also included statewide prohibition and the creation of a state highway commission, a pardon board, a board of bar examiners, state
limestone crushing plants which sold fertilizer to farmers at
cost, a tuberculosis sanitarium, and a reform school for
whites. Bilbo abolished the notorious fee system of compensating county officials—which would persist for another decade and more in some states—in favor of regular salary
scales. He sponsored a school equalization fund, expanded
school systems, and systematized new extension and adult
education courses. When "The Man" left office, however,
Mississippi's public services still lagged hopelessly behind
other states. And insofar as he could control his reforms, he
left blacks out entirely from his programs. Nevertheless,
Bilbo was by far the most effective southern mass leader
before Huey P. Long.

Across the river in Arkansas, the picturesque—sometimes
picaresque, as well—antitrust fanatic Jeff Davis entertained
the uplanders and baited Delta aristocrats, the "high collared
roosters" of the cities, and Wall Street. Dubbed by Rupert
Vance the "Karl Marx for Hill Billies," Davis as state attorney general was unlike other rustic rousers; he refused to
accept the inevitability of corporate influence in Arkansas's
affairs and interpreted quite literally the antitrust gospel. He
filed 126 suits against fire insurance companies alone and,
for good measure, took on the tobacco, cotton oil, and
freight-express "trusts." The resultant shock waves hit New
York and London and reverberated back to Little Rock, where
infuriated business leaders threatened Davis and where the
courts overruled him. Jeff took his case to the people and was
elected governor on the antitrust issue. In the end, however,
Wall Street and the corporate leviathans proved mightier
than Davis. There was no acceptable escape from Arkansas'

colonial status. Davis was a charismatic fellow; yet he must be counted as only another defeated critic of the seemingly monolithic bigness of the new industrial order.

In New York, the House of Morgan and its allies slowly consolidated Yankee control over southern railroads. Despite the South's prideful sensibilities and men such as Jeff Davis, they achieved control by the turn of the century. In the nation's capital, meanwhile, Theodore Roosevelt discriminated between "good" and "bad trusts," exempting the former from Sherman Act prosecution. The president also regularly consorted with Morgan's managers. In 1907, Roosevelt assented to U.S. Steel's (a Morgan corporation) assumption of control over the Birmingham coal and steel complex. The following year Roosevelt established his Bureau of Corporations, an ancestor of Wilson's Federal Trade Commission which was ostensibly designed to help hunt down the trusts. However, most corporations found sympathetic understanding there and a powerful base from which to design a secure, rational economy. The political power of large corporations increased nationally—while Jeff Davis, Vardaman, Bilbo, and fellow rural "Marxes" roamed the gullied hills and shouted for economic democracy.[2]

In Texas during the 1890s, rural Democrat James S. Hogg co-opted Populist issues and as governor presented a familiar reform program: improved education, farmer relief, a tough state regulatory commission for corporations. Like Davis, he embroiled the state in spectacular antitrust suits and, at one point in 1895, he sought the arrest of John D. Rockefeller and other oil magnets as fugitives from Lone Star justice. However, like Tillman, Hogg soon mellowed and drifted into a comfortable relationship with his erstwhile corporate antagonists; frustrated farmers and reformers had to look elsewhere for leadership. James E. "Farmer Jim" Ferguson, a small banker from Temple, finally emerged as a formidable successor and a spokesman for the desperate landless. Ferguson took office as governor in 1914 on a platform of sharecropper rent control, state agricultural warehouses,

penal reform, and better schools. His attempt at farmer relief was sincere and ambitious, but his tenant law proved
unenforcible and finally ran afoul of the courts. In the meantime, Ferguson's shady dealings with state funds led to his
impeachment and conviction at the hands of the legislature.
By that time, avowedly progressive reform—insofar as it remained recognizable in Texas—had all but succumbed to the
divisive prohibition issue, to Ferguson's cult of personality,
and to the lure of home-grown socialism.[3]

Rural socialism was the ultimate expression of southwestern frustration and antitrust radicalism. Affiliated with
the national Socialist party under Eugene Debs's leadership
and tinged with European radical syndicalist doctrine, the
country socialism of Louisiana, Arkansas, Texas and Oklahoma was based, nevertheless, more on a populist style of
protest than on an elaborate or articulate dogma. During
Huey Long's boyhood, it was strong in the desolate upcountry parishes of Louisiana and in neighboring Arkansas.
In 1911, a socialist Renters' Union flourished in Waco, Texas.
But rural socialism was most rampant in East Texas and in
Oklahoma, particularly in the cotton-growing southeastern
part of the new state. There, secret radical groups with violent philosophies—such as the syndicalist Working Class
Union and the bizarre Jones Family—operated alongside the
socialist Land League. Before the 1912 national elections,
the larger Land League merged with the Waco Renters'
Union. The 1914 cotton market collapse led Oklahoma Socialists to offer a full statewide slate of candidates, to propose
a program of state aid to agriculture, and to hint menacingly
at the importation of the Mexican Revolution. The slate
polled more than 50,000 votes. In 1916, despite Wilson's
peace stand and his own reform achievements, the Sooner
radicals attracted more than 42,000 votes for the Socialist
presidential candidate. During the war the southwestern
Socialists fell victim to a national xenophobic binge and
never recovered from the stigma of "bolshevist" disloyalty.
So died, temporarily at least, another futile protest, a protest

more bitter and less traditional and racial than anywhere else in the South, yet still akin to the crusades of Jeff Davis, Jim Ferguson, and their brethren to the east.

Violence beset and frequently consumed reform throughout the South, particularly rural movements in the most depressed areas. In 1903, William E. Gonzales, fiery editor of the Columbia, South Carolina, *State,* was publicly confronted and murdered by the lieutenant-governor of the state. Tennessee's vitriolic Democratic gubernatorial primary of 1908 resulted in the victory of conservative Malcolm R. Patterson over prohibitionist-reformer Edward R. Carmack. Just after the election, an associate of Patterson gunned down Carmack within sight of the state capitol in Nashville. Legislative and party pandemonium broke out. Carmack's dry friends pressed through a prohibition bill over Patterson's veto and then bolted the party to elect Republican "progressive" Ben Hooper as Patterson's successor.

In Kentucky, violence nearly destroyed the fabric of government itself. At the turn of the century, state senator William Goebel, champion antagonist of the Louisville and Nashville Railroad, campaigned for the governorship with the assistance of William Jennings Bryan and the sympathy of antitrusters everywhere. Assailing Republicans and conservative Democratic opponents for their connections with Wall Street mogul August Belmont, director of the L & N, Goebel came close to victory but lost by a narrow margin to Republican William S. Taylor. When Goebel's supporters challenged the electoral proceedings, charging fraud, Kentucky drew perilously close to civil war. While the L & N shipped in a trainload of armed mountain men, the Democratic majority in the assembly forced Taylor out of the capital. Then—on January 13, 1900, as Goebel approached the capitol—he was mortally wounded by shots fired from the office window of a Republican official. Removed to a hotel room nearby, Goebel was proclaimed governor by the Democrats, but he died four days later. The Democrats thereupon "inaugurated" his lieutenant-governor, and the commonwealth had two govern-

ments until the courts finally decided in favor of the Democrats. The accused assassin of Goebel—who three years earlier
had killed another political opponent in a pistol shoot-out—
was never convicted. Thereafter, the antitrust movement in
Kentucky bogged down in sluggish litigation which worked
in favor of the L & N.

Violence less blatantly political but equally deadly plagued
the southern masses, frustrating and diverting their efforts
to thwart economic opponents and to better their lives. Early
in the century, for example, a development company gained
title to the Reelfoot Lake area in northwest Tennessee. Local
settlers reacted with outrage at the prospective ending of
their idyllic independence by an "outside" power. In 1908,
the settlers resorted to nightriding, physical intimidation, and
finally murder in their attempt to drive the company away.
The militia finally ended the violence and the state government ultimately assumed control of the area. Similar vigilante
activity in Mississippi, fueled by racial feeling, erupted between 1902 and 1906. Because they were bitter against lien
merchants and absentee landowners who rented to and financed black tenant farmers, whites took to "whitecapping"—
a Lower South term for nightriding violence. The White-
cappers wanted to control the blacks and strike out at town
businessmen who seemed to manipulate rural affairs. Country whites were frightened by the very presence of black
landholders and renters without local white "supervision,"
and they were also angry when merchant-planters used black
laborers on their plantations, "depriving" resident white
farmers of labor. James K. Vardaman probably encouraged
Whitecapper vengeance by his virulent 1903 gubernatorial
campaign but, once in the seat of power, he hired Pinkerton
detectives and helped to subvert and destroy the movement.

Whitecapping—which occurred on a smaller scale in nearby
states—was symptomatic of the racial tensions which so often
sidetracked notable efforts at reform. Although the issue of
race supplied the impetus for certain reforms (a theme to be
developed in later chapters), it perverted and sapped other

reformist energies. Race-baiting demagoguery, whitecapping, and lynching were grossly wasteful emotional outlets which all too often corrupted rural crusades and doomed them almost from the start. As a young Populist, Tom Watson had preached against the division of poor people by race, perceiving that such division served the plutocrats' efforts at control. But, like other potentially effective reformers, his youthful balance gave way to frustration and hatred. Racial antagonisms and economic deprivation fed upon and nourished one another in a vicious, seemingly unbreakable circle.

Violence itself seemed a striking expression of the southern lifestyle. Yet, existing statistics indicate that its bloody mischief might have existed had there been no blacks. South Carolina, Kentucky, and Texas whites killed far more frequently than blacks. Also, whites generally killed whites more often than they killed blacks. Rural poor whites did not monopolize homocidal mayhem, either; low country towns were the scene of more knifings and gunplay than the red hills and the Hatfield-McCoy high country. And the newspapers of the late nineteenth and early twentieth centuries were filled with accounts of duels, shoot-outs, and dirk-swinging affrays between country gentlemen, businessmen, and professionals (including ministers)—often over the pettiest of issues. Gerald M. Capers recalled his father packing a pistol every day for weeks in Memphis during the 1920s, following a silly dispute between his child and a neighbor's. Comparing the southern homicide rate with those of Massachusetts, New England, and Italy, C. Vann Woodward concluded that the South was one of the most violent regions of comparable size in Western Civilization. It is possible, although not provable, that even white-versus-white violence had roots in the excessively prideful sense of self-sovereignty engendered by the ideology of white supremacy. It has also been suggested that southerners brought up their children in such a manner as to encourage aggressiveness (as opposed to suicide, a statistically rare event below the Potomac). Nevertheless, whatever the varied and numerous causes, the persistent channeling of energies into nonproductive violence became a tragic theme in the region.

Rarely, violence did abet reform. By the turn of the century, James B. "Buck" Duke, the only genuine Gilded Age "robber baron" produced by the South, had forged a monopoly in his American Tobacco Company. Duke used his power to force down leaf tobacco prices to below the farmers' cost of production. The most vigorous response came from dark leaf growers in the Black Patch, a block of counties on either side of the border between central Kentucky and Tennessee. In 1904, these growers organized a Planters' Protective Association which included both landowners and tenant farmers. They first attempted to use political leverage and to force American Tobacco to bargain with them. Then they built cooperatively owned warehouses and attempted to create their own market with fair prices. Finally, frustrated by the ennui of Kentucky politics and by the power of Duke, they took to horse, gun, and faggot in 1906. Blatantly revolutionary in method, the Black Patch warriors dynamited or burned ATC-owned factories and warehouses; they destroyed seedbeds and blew up barns belonging to "trust" collaborators; and, in order further to compel virtual unanimity among burley growers, they horsewhipped, sometimes murdered, men and women, slaughtered livestock, and shot up houses.

The spirit of uprising and antitrust incendiarism spread southward to cotton states and there combined momentarily with whitecapping. It seemed, by 1908, that a general rural revolt might be at hand but, when Kentucky state troops finally ended the Black Patch War, the other rumblings of revolution also sputtered out. Meanwhile, tobacco manufacturers and retailers agreed to deal with bargainers representing burley growers in Kentucky and several surrounding states and, for a few years, farmers' prices remained equitable. The farmers had won their original goal but at a terrific cost.

Much of the southern antimonopoly movement took more respectable and less revolutionary forms, however. From 1896 until he became Wilson's Secretary of the Navy in 1913, Josephus Daniels of North Carolina was probably the outstanding southern antitrust crusader. A clean-cut, ambitious, hyperactive young man, in the early 1890s he served as chief clerk of the Department of Interior in the second Cleveland administration. He soon deserted to the cause of rural insurgent William Jennings Bryan, whom Daniels enthusiastically described as "the young David from Nebraska" out to slay the plutocratic "Goliath." In 1898, Daniels headed the journalistic department of the Democratic white supremacy campaign in his home state—researching and publishing inflammatory racial exposes of the Republican-Populist government and of black politicians' "insults" to white women. His Raleigh *News and Observer* was probably more important than any other organ in provoking white vigilanteeism and rousing the Red Shirts, self-appointed paramilitary enforcers of "white man's rule." Once the Democrats were back in power under Governor Charles B. Aycock, Daniels crusaded for virtually all "progressive" causes: public education, prohibition, clean government, and especially the regulation of railroads and other corporations.[5]

In 1907, Daniels, assembly House Speaker Edward J. Justice, and State Senator Reuben Reid stood at their armageddon. Together they plotted and executed a legislative campaign to reduce railway passenger rates to a uniform two cents per mile, a rate consistent with that current in other states, including neighboring Virginia. The railroads and their allies fought back stoutly. Daniels counterattacked. He exposed a senator whom a Southern Railway vice president had paid to vote against the proposed bill and proved that the railroad had also subsidized a rival newspaper. Meanwhile, Justice and Reid, both masterful legislators, guided through by close margins in each house a law establishing a two and a quarter cent uniform rate—according to Daniels, "the most brilliant victory in the history of legislation in North Carolina, in all the time I have observed Legislatures." However, some of the carriers, led by the Southern, were successful in obtaining a federal court injunction, a favorite and time-honored tactic to circumvent state regulation. Daniels thereupon rallied the public in red-letter headlines and commanded state officials to indict the railroad managers and to ignore the federal magistrate. Governor Robert B. Glenn rattled the state's rusty nullification sabres; the North Carolina superior court defied the injunction, indicted, and actually ordered the imprisonment of a Southern agent for selling tickets above the rate established by the recent law. State officers also arrested the Southern's president and other road officials, and the court handed them heavy fines. However, an impending, climactic crisis in federal-state relations finally gave way to compromise. A state court remitted the rail officials' fines, and a special session of the legislature accepted a regular passenger rate of two and one half cents per mile. Most importantly, the Southern and other lines accepted state authority at last.

The inland giant, the Louisville and Nashville, did not bow so quickly. This line's intransigent president, Milton Hannibal Smith, battled Braxton Bragg Comer—a businessman elected governor of Alabama in 1907 on an antitrust platform—to a standstill. A former railroad commissioner, Comer led the legislature in strengthening the railroad commission and substantially lowering both passenger and freight rates. Then, after the final curtain of the North Carolina drama, the L & N played an Alabama encore, including bribery and newspaper subsidies. The railroad had an extraordinary ally in Alabama: the local federal judge, Thomas G. Jones, who happened to be a former L & N attorney. Jones not only enjoined most of the new railroad acts but invalidated the state's "ouster law," which revoked the licenses of foreign corporations that sued the state. He further declared the railroad commission's rate-making power unconstitutional. When the legislature responded with an "injunction proof" law which required the courts to enjoin every citizen of the state, Judge Jones, upon application by Smith, did precisely that—confounding one absurdity with another.

The persistent Smith carried on his defiance of Alabama law after both Comer and Jones had retired from office. In 1913, the L & N finally capitulated. By that time federal legislation (the Physical Valuation Act) gave them little choice; so at long last, moderate antitrustism met with moderate success.

Walter Clark—a southern patrician, North Carolina supreme court justice and, for two decades, an advanced spokesman for reform—was on the periphery of these rate battles and a darling of monopoly-fighters everywhere. Clark's prime interest was antitrustism, but his wide-ranging opinions on many issues galled strict constructionist colleagues on the state high court. For example, he advocated from the bench a graduated income tax for public school support. He arbitrarily inserted into another judicial opinion his study of nations and American states employing the franchise tax on public service corporations, and he concluded with the frank suggestion that North Carolina adopt such a tax. Clark also promoted compulsory school attendance laws, tough factory inspection in anti-child-labor programs, workmen's compensation, and woman's suffrage. Responding to critics, Clark had the temerity to declare that "every civilized government is to a large extent, and almost in proportion to its degree of civilization, socialistic." Indeed, Clark's increasing preoccupation with the rights and protection of children, women, and workers carried him well beyond the concerns of most southern antitrust reformers.

Edward J. Justice, whom Daniels himself called the "Progressive of Progressives" was far more typical and revealing of the rural reform consensus. Justice was the leading reform agitator in the legislature in the great antirailway session of 1907; he also introduced an antitrust law "with teeth" that year. Justice was also around later to lead the house in the 1913 legislature—known as the greatest reform session in North Carolina history. A critic of all trusts, from railroads to Duke's Southern Power Company, Justice sought a state corrupt practices law and, in 1913, was finally successful in strengthening the power of the corporation commission to fix rates, prevent discrimination, and prohibit rebates by utilities. He was a proponent of compulsory school attendance, free medical and dental examinations for school children, and free textbooks. In 1913, he also attempted to win state constitutional amendments securing the initiative and referendum, and he succeeded in persuading the house to pass resolutions inviting Woodrow Wilson, William Jennings Bryan, and Robert M. La Follette to speak in Raleigh in behalf of these democratizing reforms.

Justice's several definitions of "progressive" reform and his explanations of his own motivation were most interesting. In 1916 he told a group of Californians that Jefferson had founded a party based on the principle of "majority rule," but that from time to time it was necessary to redemocratize the party and the nation. Justice said that Andrew Jackson performed such a duty, fighting "special interests," notably the monopolistic Bank of the United States. In the 1912 elections, he continued, "the issues were strikingly similar to those upon which Jackson defeated Clay. . . . History is repeating itself in a remarkable degree." Yet, the issue of centralization versus state rights concerned Justice as much as the struggle between "the people" and "special interests"; indeed, to him, there was hardly any difference: morality lay with democracy (the people) and with state rights, a governmental philosophy which he felt best represented democracy. In 1909, he wrote to Bryan that two years earlier he "had gone to the legislature largely because Mr. [Elihu] Root and Mr. Roosevelt were teaching the doctrine of centralization by saying that the states were impotent to regulate the public service corporations, or to destroy the trusts." Justice's role, then, was the desperate effort to maintain local control in the hands of moral, middle class leaders such as himself— before the systematizers and centralizers, such as Theodore Roosevelt and the interstate businessmen, could grab power. However, in the age of the triumph of rationalization and centralism Justice was doomed to frustration. "The growth of the sentiment in favor of centralized government at Washington is due, more than anything else, to the failure of state legislatures to intelligently and bravely exercise their constitutional powers to correct abuses, and the failure of state prosecuting officers and courts to enforce the law against the rich and powerful."[6]

Virtually all southern antitrust reformers were of this moderate bent, unless—like the Black Patch riders and the southwestern radicals—desperation drove them to revolutionary action or centralist ideologies. Such upright, middle-class men as Justice, Daniels, and Comer were fundamentally antirevolutionary, conserving people. The theme holds true despite rich variations of social origins and factional affiliations. Virginia's respectable "education governor," Andrew Jackson Montague, for example, played the antimachine insurgent role in state politics, but he differed hardly at all from factional enemies in his devotion to white supremacy, rule by the "best people," and state rights. North Carolina's counterpart to Montague, Charles B. Aycock, another young campaigner for white supremacy and educational reform, was the fair-haired boy of the business-oriented machine of U.S. Senator Furnifold M. Simmons.[7]

Florida's "progressive" governor, Napoleon Bonaparte Broward, descended from an antebellum upper-class family, impoverished by the war. As a boy and young man, he worked aboard boats on the St. Johns River, off Newfoundland, and out of Boston as a steward and deck hand. Returning to Florida, he river-piloted and skippered his own steamer. At thirty-three (1888), he was elected sheriff of Duval County (surrounding Jacksonville) and served until the mid-1890s, when he began running guns to Cuban revolutionaries. His adventures brought him fame and a political career. Ever mindful of his early hardships and consequently sympathizing with the poor and aspiring, he became a Bryan-style champion of the common white man by attacking barriers of "privilege." Railroads and land development companies were special targets and, like Daniels, Justice, Comer and antitrusters in other states, he did battle before the legislatures and courts. Broward's obsession, however, was a project to drain the Everglades and create a Florida frontier with cheap land for all the crackers. By this means, traditional values and opportunities threatened by "land pirates" and trusts might be preserved.

South Carolina aristocrats Duncan Clinch Heyward and Richard I. Manning present further variations of the traditional struggle for reform. Heyward, obscure seigneur of "Myrtle Grove," a low country rice plantation, was chosen governor in 1902 as a peace candidate between warring Democratic factions. Courtly, Virginia-educated, and moderate, he paid necessary homage to Tillman while gaining the confidence of old bourbon types such as himself. Heyward's administration emphasized longer school terms, good roads, and mild child labor legislation—paving the way toward the climactic reform tenure of Manning (1915–1919), who was a planter-lawyer-businessman and scion of a leading political family. Patrician Manning's governorship resembled and rivaled that of the Mississippi plebeian Bilbo. He and legislators revised and equalized South Carolina's tax structure; established compulsory school attendance (although on a local option basis); passed effective child labor control and workers' hours and pay laws; created a board of arbitration to settle labor disputes; and founded a highway commission, a board of charities and corrections, and various social welfare institutions. In addition, Manning attempted unsuccessfully to provide inexpensive loans to tenants wishing to buy farm land.

This conserving or restorative impulse also guided such different men as Henry St. George Tucker and G. Walter Mapp of Virginia. Tucker, scholarly prince of an Old Dominion family prominent since before the Revolution, was an out-of-place early nineteenth-century constitutional lawyer. Tucker was a congressman for a time during the 1890s and subsequently dean of the law school at Washington and Lee University. He saw himself as one of the "best people" and desperately, pathetically, sought offices year after year, hop-

ing to appear all the while a disinterested statesman of the
old school. Tucker's ideal was a scrupulously honest, spare,
efficient government which did essentially nothing except
police a strictly construed constitutional regime. He was a
trustbusting decentralizer but, unlike most traditionalists, he
opposed prohibition. Tucker was sympathetic to the child
labor reform movement but, of course, opposed federal regulation even of this abuse. He could not bear majoritarian
coercion, and his extreme, strict constructionist interpretation
of the constitution precluded his endorsement of virtually all
positive, centralist legislation. Tucker was one of those
grandly ineffective and irrelevant southern gentlemen, a
"progressive" by virtue of his decent instincts, political insurgency, and powerful desire to conserve what he conceived
to be an idyllic, noble past.

G. Walter Mapp, on the other hand, was a dynamic provincial entrepreneur and a moral authoritarian. A farmer, businessmen, and organizer of rural utilities companies in Ac-
comac County on the Eastern Shore, Mapp came from a strict
Methodist background. His hard-working qualities and his
devotion to social duty and to reform were no doubt strengthened by his long friendship and association with the Reverend James Cannon, Jr., a fellow Methodist and the architect
of statewide prohibition in Virginia. After being elected to
the state senate in 1911, Mapp chose for himself the mantle,
"leader of moral forces in the legislature." In addition to the
prohibition law, which bore his name, he sponsored bills to
abolish the death penalty, to exorcise brothels, and to establish a motion picture censorship board—all of which failed.
However, Mapp's other reform efforts were successful: he
sponsored the establishment of a legislative reference bureau
and a tough state antitrust law.

It is revealing that the impotent reformer Tucker was an
insurgent and that Mapp, able and successful, was a member
of the "conservative" machine of Senator Thomas S. Martin.
Indeed, the examples of both Virginia and North Carolina
illustrate the weakness of such labels as "insurgent," "con-

servative," and "progressive" as indicators of reform and antireform political skirmish lines. Virginia reform governor Montague, an antimachine insurgent, was followed by Martin machine candidate Claude A. Swanson, whose work in behalf of education and good roads surpassed his predecessor's. Swanson's machine successor, William H. Mann, was also a consummate "progressive" reformer. In North Carolina, reform reached its apex during the activist administration of Locke Craig, a minion of the Simmons organization. During Craig's tenure the assembly—also machine dominated—enacted a compulsory school attendance law, provided for six month schools and stricter factory inspection in the child labor program, and established the direct primary. Craig was more successful than his antimachine predecessor, William W. Kitchen, for the very reason that Virginia's Swanson was effective in moderate reform: both men represented political organizations which commanded loyalty from legislatures. They eschewed obstinancy for the sake of partisanship. It is beyond question that many state "bosses" such as Martin and Simmons aligned themselves with "New South" industrialists and enjoyed a cozy relationship with the "foreign" railroads; yet, both presided over loose, flexible, pragmatic "machines," and both had the wisdom to recognize the necessity of bending before the winds of reform sentiment. Thus, even the most "reactionary" of political machines usually accommodated moderate antitrustism, demands for public services, and moral crusades which did little to disturb the basic economic and social order. Beneath the tumult of radicalism, racial extremism, and violence, most "progressive" reform came about ultimately at the sufferance of shrewd men interested mainly in their own continued control.

III

UP WITH HUMANITY – AND EXPERTS

But Progressivism after all is more a spirit than a creed. It means the restoration of the government to the people.

WALTER HINES PAGE, 1912

Successful government requires the same principles applied as does successful business.

WESTMORELAND DAVIS, 1922

A variety of urban, social welfare, and public service reformers were seldom completely separate from the antimonopoly reformers. Some of these social reformers were reactionary members of the elite who wished to reassert their values and regain their lost control. Many were paternalistic "uplifters," dreamers and decentralizers. Other city reformers were "experts," professionals, and centralizers with competent "scientific" cures for social, economic, and political ills. Bigotry cut across class and reform-style lines: certain reformers were actuated to "do good" by racial obsessions; others played out their roles beyond the realm of the color question. Working parallel with—and sometimes opposed to—rural and town-based crusaders, the urban reformers further illustrate, in their rich diversity, the ferment of change in the South before World War I.

Virtually every southern city had its set of patricians-for-clean-government. In New Orleans a typical "best people's" Good Government League attempted to break the power of Choctaw Club boss Martin Behrman. The antimachine reformers, who were mainly wealthy Protestants such as John M. Parker, J. Y. Sanders, and Jean Gordon, couched their goals and grievances in class and ethnic terms. Gordon wrote to Parker in early 1911: "We have to break up this unholy Alliance which seems to be growing between Catholic and Jew in office holding. . . . Personally I have no objections to Catholics . . . [or] Jews, but when the Catholic in his great numbers and the Jew with his control of the money situation make a combine it is a hard thing to have better conditions." She especially deplored the "jesuitical principle of the 'end justifying the means'," a device beneath the disinterested spirit of the League. Gordon, Parker, and their friends intended to achieve better conditions through elite Protestant rule and "efficient" government.[1]

In Charleston, low country aristocrat Robert Goodwyn Rhett led the antivice, good government battles; he was another mugwump out to save the people from themselves. A corps of civic club women from the cream of society joined Rhett and his colleagues in civic betterman campaigns. Established in 1900 by Cristie Poppenheim, the Civic Club of Charleston undertook important social projects often beneath the notice of men. Mitchell Playground, the first urban park for children in the state, was an early accomplishment. A recreation club for working girls, enforcement of health regulations in schools, an ordinance requiring lids on garbage cans, and myriad public art and beautification projects followed. These did not disturb the fundamental class structure and poverty of Charleston, but the ladies' amateur efforts in "sociology" and public health laid the basis for later effective, professional attention.

Baltimore possessed a reformer-aristocrat of undoubted

credentials in Charles J. Bonaparte, a grandson of the emperor's brother Jerome and scion of a local corporate dynasty. A Catholic, Harvardian, Republican, intimate of Theodore Roosevelt and sometime presidential cabinet member— Bonaparte as a young man in the 1870s joined the national civil service reform movement and, in the mid-1880s, turned to reform in his own city by organizing the Baltimore Reform League. Associated with Bonaparte were Daniel Coit Gilman, the New England patrician who became president of the Johns Hopkins University; Virginia-born William Cabell Bruce, partner in an elite law firm and a reform Democratic state senator; and Charles H. Grasty, another Virginian, who was crusading editor of the *Baltimore Evening News*. In the early 1890s, Grasty began to publicize Reform League projects and boost civil betterment. At first, Grasty, Bonaparte, and friends attacked the traction and utilities companies for their high rates and poor service. They then assailed the Democratic, machine-run city administration for neglecting to clean streets and to inspect the slum areas. The League also exposed the numbers racket and local sweatshops. Gilman and some of his associates went beyond alms-giving in their charity work and paved the way for an environmental emphasis in their approach to social problems.

After 1900, the Baltimore reformers fought the effort by Democratic boss Arthur P. Gorman to disfranchise blacks. Gorman not only sought to carry the southern disfranchisement movement into Maryland; he attempted to undo a Baltimore reform coalition of rich, white Republicans, mugwump Democratic enemies, and poor, largely illiterate blacks. Posing as a reformer himself—like most disfranchisers—Gorman proposed constitutional amendments which included the literacy test and a grandfather clause in 1903. (At this time the assembly was also passing a raft of Jim Crow laws.) However, in Maryland, disfranchisement failed. In both 1905 and 1908, voters rejected Gorman's measures, and in Maryland there were no effective paramilitary forces to bulldoze blacks without restraint, as in Mississippi and the Carolinas.

Baltimore and environs were almost unique in the South because reform remained separate from racial extremism. However, the situation owed more to circumstances than to sentiment: Republicans needed black voters; the substantial number of foreign-born whites in the city feared literacy tests and voted with the blacks against electoral "reform;" and unlike the Catholic hierarchy in New Orleans, Baltimore's church, led by the courageous Cardinal Francis Gibbons, actively opposed disfranchisement. Thus, Baltimore's heterogeneity and healthy two party system helped block the racial reforms so omnipresent in the rest of the South.

In Richmond, much as in Charleston, patricians and women dominated the reform movements. In 1900, city gentlefolk founded the Richmond Education Association, which was led by Ben and Lila Meade Valentine and Beverley and Mary Cooke Branch Munford. Lila Valentine and Mary Munford, both former city belles, were active in numerous civic campaigns and were the first two presidents of the Education Association. They and their spouses were interested in revitalizing old values and in managing improvements for blacks. In 1903, they began the city's first kindergarten, then saw to the institution of industrial training in black schools, fire drills and inspection, and the construction of a new white high school. Their work, meanwhile, joined with that of the Southern Education Board and soon merged with a strong rural crusade for schools.

Rollicking, murderous, jazzy Memphis also had its patricians, but the river city's most significant "progressive" phenomenon was Edward Hull Crump. Crump descended from Virginia and Mississippi planters; his father had served as a lieutenant in Morgan's Confederate Raiders and had planted cotton at Holly Springs, Mississippi, near Memphis. However, unlike the Rhetts, Bonapartes, and Valentines, Crump's style and goals were not the shedding of seigneurial grace upon the masses or the reassertion of his class's

prestige and leadership. Growing up fatherless from the
age of four, surrounded by genteel poverty, Crump developed
a sense of drive and, in the words of his biographer, "a
passion for order." "Plan your work and work your plan"
was Crump's favorite maxim. He set out for Memphis in
1894 to win success in the business world and, by 1900,
was the secretary-treasurer of a carriage and saddlery
business. Not long afterward, he owned his own buggy company and later an insurance brokerage as well. In his career
as clerk, cashier, and executive, Crump thoroughly learned
the ways of good business and became intolerant of inefficiency and waste. His gregariousness and his tall, red-haired,
and dimpled good looks swept him into politics. He carried
his passion for systematization and economy with him.

Crump was impatient with the easy-going corruption of
Memphis public affairs under the regime of J. J. Williams,
an old-style boss. As a ward politician and councilman,
Crump learned of contract favoritism, graft, nepotism, and
incompetence. As a police and fire commissioner, he chaffed
at the administration's refusal to stifle vice and at the lack
of professionalism in the police department. Factional politics, he decided, had to be divorced from public administration. In 1909, then, he successfully campaigned for both the
office of mayor and the commission form of government.
He took office on New Year's Day, 1910. Mayor Crump was
honest, refused favors, drove vice safely within the confines
of the black ghetto, saw to the employment of competent
bureaucrats, and opened public bids on costly purchases
of city supplies and on contract work. He systematized and
extended public health, which had been a scandal in the
squalid river town, and he pledged himself to the creation
of publicly owned utilities.

Crump competed with his opponents in his devotion to
white supremacy. In his 1909 campaign, he personally struck
a Negro holding a ballot marked for his opponent. Yet, in
most other respects, Crump was hardly a typical southern
mayor; he represented, instead a new American middle class

that carried the style and techniques of business into public administration. Like others in the North, he brought experts into government and overthrew the inefficiency, corruption, and affable equalitarianism of the old bosses. Crump and his Memphis were unique, to be sure, but his regime displayed bureaucratic reform similar to San Francisco, Toledo, Cleveland, and dozens of other cities across the country.

This obsession with control and efficiency spread—not only to other southern cities but to states and even to smaller provincial towns. This fettish for business-like government reached its peak in the 1920s. The commission form of city government, for example, with its emphasis upon administration by experts, originated in Galveston following the great hurricane and tidal wave of 1900. The inefficient council form of government was not adequate for the task of rebuilding; therefore, professionals assumed the jobs of administering sewerage, fire and police protection, and lights and traffic. In 1903, Houston followed Galveston's example; then Dallas and a half dozen other Texas cities. The commission movement spread eastward to New Orleans, Jackson, Birmingham, Charlotte, and Memphis—as young executive-types like Crump demanded the same competence in public affairs as in business.

In 1908, Staunton, Virginia, first implemented the city-manager plan, an alternate form of urban government-by-experts. This, too, spread across the country. However, subsequently both plans became identified with northern cities—the "Des Moines Idea" and the "Dayton Idea"—since southerners apparently lacked in promotional impetus what they possessed in innovation. Another centralizing device, the short ballot, spread to hundreds of southern towns and cities during the progressive era. By means of it, the public usually elected only a mayor and council, who made policy and appropriated funds. This eliminated from the elective process such officials as school superintendents and police chiefs, who were now hired for their expertise by the council and were responsible to the council.

At the state level, corporate-style centralization gained momentum with the rewriting of constitutions. Along with electoral "purification" the disfranchisers frequently undertook to clear up bureaucratic jumbles and to grant more power to their governors. Virginia's "business governor," Westmoreland Davis, borrowed the best features of Wisconsin's and California's executive budget plans and, in 1918, the assembly adopted his "Virginia Plan." This plan replaced the notoriously inefficient legislative budgeting system common to most states. By 1922, Davis's executive budget system had been employed by eight other states—three in the South and five in the West. Typically, Davis saw himself as director of a corporation.

Alabama's governor, Thomas E. Kilby, a prohibitionist and candidate of the Anti-Saloon League in 1918, agreed with Davis on administrative matters. A shrewd Anniston steel manufacturer, he established an executive budget, then systematized the state school system and penitentiary. Charles Hillman Brough, a Johns Hopkins trained economist and an active sociologist, resigned his professorship at the University of Arkansas to win that state's governorship in 1916. Virtually the antithesis of Jeff Davis in style and approach, Brough brought "respectability" and the regimen of an efficiency expert to the Southwest. Westmoreland Davis, Kilby, and Brough hastened the centralist trend in state administration which, like urban counterparts, would flourish in the 1920s.

Another popular administrative device was the legislative reference bureau. First made famous in Wisconsin and New Jersey, these lawmakers' reference aids were established in a number of southern states and in some larger cities. The essential functions of the bureaus were comparative data collection, research, and expert assistance in bill drafting for legislators—with the emphasis upon "expert." In Virginia and North Carolina, for example, farmers and insurgent groups first proposed legislative reference bureaus with the rationale that the bureaus would make possible the ascendancy of non-lawyer legislators. The editor of the *Southern Planter* (Richmond) called upon the electorate to "keep your constitutional lawyers and politicians at home and send some progressive farmer to make laws for you." Presumably the reference bureau's experts could make unprofessional legislators competent. The central bureau became an answer to the problem of restoring democracy in an age of centralization.

Southerners also moved toward professionalism and bureaucratic efficiency in the area of social welfare. As late as the turn of the century, responsibility for amelioration remained in the hands of the traditional laymen who headed urban charitable organizations and state commissions of charities and corrections. Then, the statewide "conference for social service," a mid-western invention, moved south. In 1900, physicians, hospital administrators, and a few amateur charity workers founded the Virginia Conference for Social Service. The members primarily discussed problems of public health and resolved to work for improved legislation. A similar conference was established in Kentucky in 1904, in South Carolina and Alabama in 1909, in Florida and Texas in 1911, and in Arkansas in 1912. Then Oklahoma's Kate Barnard and Tennessee's reform Republican Ben Hooper called a great Southern Sociological Congress, which met in Nashville in 1912. More than 700 delegates came from fifteen southern states and discussed a wide range of southern problems—from child labor to prisons to race relations. The delegates were mixed: socially aware politicians such as Hooper; Barnard, who was both a consummate politician and an experienced social worker; Clarence Poe, owner-editor of the *Progressive Farmer* (Raleigh); academicians such as Charles Hillman Brough of Arkansas; and a raft of preachers. Some of the professionals thought the Congress "too damned pious;" there was even an official Congress "Battle Hymn," sung to the tune of "Tipperary." However, professionals dominated the Congress as well as later state conferences; these conferences became in turn even more powerful platforms for political action. The professionalization of social work continued in a lively climate.[2]

The emergence of dynamic women professionals materially furthered reform in several areas. After a northern education in John Dewey's "progressive" teaching methods, Virginia-born Celest Parrish introduced the new pedagogy to Georgia. Following years of training teachers at the State Normal School, she became rural education supervisor in North Georgia, riding the country circuit in her buggy. Parrish's contemporary, Alabamian Julia Tutwiler, founded her state's normal college for women and went on to lead compaigns for penal reform and the improvement of children's educa-tion. Harriet Morehead Berry of North Carolina also taught. She left a later position as a stenographer for the State Geological and Economic Survey to become the executive secretary of the Good Roads Association; here, she worked to create a state-supported highway network, which was finally adopted largely through her efforts.

Methodist laywomen initiated the social settlement move-ment in the South. Striving at once for "uplift" and profes-sional expertise, they organized "home missions" in Atlanta and other cities for aiding the poor, and then went on to found a system of private welfare agencies, low-cost boarding houses for women workers, community recreation centers, and rural missions. In 1911, Mary DeBardelaban of Alabama moved to Augusta, Georgia in order to work with Negroes. There, she organized a settlement house program, Sunday school, kindergarten, and black Civic Improvement League. By 1916, the southern Methodist women's Missionary Council had formally adopted a manifold activist program; the aboli-tion of child labor and illiteracy, prison reform, and improved race relations headed their list.

The social welfare and service reformers of both sexes accomplished much in the South. Penal reform was one of their most fruitful labors. After Reconstruction, southern politicos had solved the problem of housing and policing prisoners with the convict-leasing system. Under this notoriously cruel method of penology, states lent convicts at bargain rates to mine owners, manufacturers, and especially to the railroads; these companies worked prisoners to death and brutalized them. Furthermore, the system bore particularly hard on blacks. Toward the end of the 1890s, critics of leasing won a sympathetic hearing, perhaps in part because major railway construction in the region was finally complete. At any rate, Mississippi led the way and abolished the institution in 1898; Louisiana, Arkansas, Texas, Georgia, and Tennessee followed before 1917. In the early 1920s, tardy Upper South states—where leasing had been less deadly —followed suit. The first alternative to leasing was prison farm work—an early version of "state use" industry—which involved important agricultural experiments. After the advent of the automobile and the creation of the first state highway commissions, roadbuilding and maintenance became the most important means of employing prisoners. In Virginia and Mississippi, convicts also worked in state-owned limestone quarries and grinding plants which produced inexpensive lime for farmers.

During the progressive years, public health reform was important nationally. Nevertheless, it had special significance in the South, where both climate and poverty bred special problems. Hookworm, a chief cause of southern "laziness," was diagnosed early in the century by local physicians. Then in 1909 a Yankee, Dr. Charles W. Stiles, inaugurated an education and eradication program in the South with the help of Rockefeller financing. Meanwhile, the International Health Board, another private agency, undertook pioneer programs against malaria—demonstrating the effectiveness of spraying, drainage, screening windows, and quinine treatment. Pellagra, another southern malady previously mistaken for laziness, was identified in 1906 at the Alabama Hospital for the Colored Insane. Eight years later, the federal public health service finally sent Dr. Joseph Goldberger to investigate. He soon identified the cause of pellagra as a simple protein deficiency. By that time (1914), every southern state had some kind of health agency, and southern counties led the nation in the number of local health departments. Some "New South" boomers, who believed the region was already healthy and prosperous, feared the effect of public health agitation on business. Yet, once established, the professional services proved popular and durable. A subtle but profound change was overtaking the region.

After 1896, the South had become the most enthusiastically antitrust section of the union. Its Democratic politicians rallied in behalf of currency inflation and antimonopoly legislation—out of sincere conviction or political necessity. During the popular presidencies of McKinley and Roosevelt, it was the South which most loyally supported Bryan and vestiges of the agrarian revolt—now called provincial insurgency and progressivism. Southern congressmen frequently voted with Republican insurgents such as La Follette and Beveridge of the Middle West.[3]

When, in 1910, Democrats took over control of Congress, southerners became even more prominent in national politics. They played key roles in seeking democratizing reforms. Alabama's Oscar Underwood and Oklahoma's Robert Owen offered early resolutions in support of the direct election of U.S. senators, although other southerners feared qualifications which might threaten their race settlement at home. Southern and western "progressives" combined to pressure candidate Woodrow Wilson, never before hostile to big business, to assume an antitrust stance. Then in the halcyon days of 1913-1914, with southerners holding the most significant committee chairmanships, Congress passed the first downward revision of the tariff in decades. Tacked onto the Underwood-Simmons Act was an implementing provision for the first income tax, which was drafted and generaled through the House by another southerner, Tennessee's Cordell Hull. Under pressure from Mississippi's Vardaman and John Nance Garner of Texas, Congress added a graduated surtax on large incomes. It also named a compre-

hensive antitrust and labor reform act for yet another
Dixie representative, Henry D. Clayton of Alabama. The
principal authorship of the Federal Reserve Act is difficult
to determine, but Virginia's cantankerous, red-haired reformer, Carter Glass, at least consulted with Wilson and
received major credit. Wilson insisted upon a central federal
reserve board of governors with banker representation, but
Glass won his main decentralizing goal—twelve regional
banks. In 1913-1914 southern and western antitrusters also
won a final regulatory law for railroads and some credit
relief—however inadequate—for farmers.

Then, the Wilson administration suddenly moved beyond
antitrustism to encompass important centralist developments.
Southerners had little part in creating the Federal Trade
Commission, which would merely regulate—not "bust"—the
trusts. However, southerners were the initiators of other
centralist bureaucratization and, ironically enough, rural representatives formed the vanguard. In 1914, Congress passed
the Cotton Warehouse Act, a mild version of the southern
Populists' subtreasury idea of the 1890s. In 1916, under
pressure from South Carolinian Asbury Francis Lever, the
Federal Farm Loan Act created a system of government-
controlled land banks which extended inexpensive long-term
loans to farmers. In the meantime, Lever and Georgia's Hoke
Smith gave their names to a law which institutionalized yet
another enduring bureau—the Agricultural Extension Service.
According to a Texas congressman, no farm measure "will
be worth the paper it is written on, which does not provide
for government aid." Here again, the central bureau was
expediently adopted by traditional state rightists and decentralizers.

In 1916 Southern legislators were almost evenly divided
on the federal child labor legislation cosponsored by Oklahoma's Robert Owen; it was dangerous and unpatriotic
for Carolinians and Georgians to gall the textile companies.
Although Georgia's William C. Adamson sponsored the Eight
Hour Act for railway workers, few southerners other than he

and Owen took much interest in labor. However, in the field of highway financing, agitation for an end to localism originated in the South. As early as 1907 John H. Bankhead won election to the Senate from Alabama, principally on a federal aid-to-roads platform. Constitutional scruples prevented other southerners from supporting Bankhead's project; however, in 1916, they succumbed to an argument that presaged the distant future: national highways were essential to national defense. The Bankhead-Shakelford Federal Highways Act provided $75 million of federal aid to states with highway departments that would match federal funds and meet federal standards. By that time, all the southern states had highway departments and master plans for road-building; now, the rural constituencies as well as the urban business types would have their roads.

Finally, southerners won another bureaucratic victory. During the Wilson years, they officially sanctioned segregation of the races in all federal agencies. This reform was primarily the work of Navy Secretary Josephus Daniels, southern-born Treasury Secretary William Gibbs McAdoo, and Postmaster General Albert Burleson of Texas. As far as practicable, they separated clerks, janitors, and other workers and installed extra restrooms. To the white officials from the South, this last reform simply reflected a fitting and consistent adjunct to what they called the "progressive movement."

IV

REFORM AND MASTERY:
A MEDLEY OF MINISTERS

Things must change in order to remain the same.

> the wise aristocrat in di Lampedusa's
> *The Leopard.*

*In our revolt from Puritanism, the Pendulum has
swung to the other extreme. [Now] we are reaping
the harvest of our criminal . . . liberalism.*

JAMES CANNON, JR., 1905

"SOCIAL control" was *au courant* among American university people and urban reformers at the turn of the century. First popularized by sociologist Edward A. Ross, the term described a means of reform: social scientists would compile data on society and then effect improvements. However, for many, social control was probably also an *end* of reform. Reformers' precise motives will ever evade historians; nevertheless, a desire to assert personal mastery and assure the place of their own kind appears to have been shared by Jane Addams, Felix Adler, John Dewey, the famous muckrakers, and others engaged

57

in "progressive" work. Social control, which was seldom
well defined and hardly conspiratorial, merely expressed the
rather smug belief among professionals—from social workers
to crusading journalists—that their expertise could bring
about better conditions and a rational new "order." Furthermore, the order-builders would earn leadership positions.[1]

Southern reformers also sought to impose new regulations
on society, in order to achieve social control. The southerners'
imperative was greater because they faced somewhat different and more complex problems than those the Yankees
confronted. Another difference was the belief of many southern reformers that they stood at the crossroads of history;
their sense of historical drama was well-founded: Confederate
veterans, Bourbon gentlemen, and "old time darkies" were
fast dying off, along with other references to the old regime.
Parts of the South were undergoing rapid growth in commerce and manufacturing: the factory-worker class, including
so many women and children, grew ever larger; and the
parvenue managers of business extended their power. Poor
white democracy was also on the rise. The rural masses—
full of class and caste consciousness and commanded by
tempestuous leaders—held the balance of power in some
states and threatened in nearly all. The great race settlement
promised security for whites, but the future for blacks themselves remained a monumental uncertainty. The South, then,
which had known convulsion before and lived with the
fear of apocalypse, had reached another crisis point in its
tumultuous history. Intrepid reformers rose to the challenge.

This chapter is about three remarkable southern clergymen
who refused to accept helplessly whatever fate might produce from these powerful new circumstances. Each sensed
his mission in history and, while each preacher was quite
different from the others, all shared a determination to
assert mastery, to guide, and to bring under some pre-
dictable control a society in flux.

❖   ❖   ❖   ❖   ❖   ❖   ❖

Sailing new seas demands reliable navigational equipment. No matter how brave and innovative a reformer might be, he needed—like any human—a familiar standard, a frame of reference. In this respect the Old South played an important conceptual function for many progressive reformers; for some, certain features of the old regime became the embodiment of their hopes for the future. This was especially the case with the Reverend Edgar Gardner Murphy (1869-1913)—a brilliant clergyman, successful social reformer, articulate spokesman for the new southern order, masterful mollifier of skeptical Yankees, and a true believer in the Old South's aristocracy.

However, for Murphy and his contemporaries, the Old South was hardly the South of Nat Turner and Simon Legree; but rather the "benevolent tyranny" pictured by Georgia-born historian Ulrich B. Phillips and by such myth-making storytellers of the 1880s and afterwards as Thomas Nelson Page of Virginia. Nearly all these writers condemned slavery as un-American and inefficient, if not immoral; except possibly Page by default, none suggested its re-establishment. What Murphy and his generation admired was the security and dependability of the social hierarchy they saw in the Old South. They particularly revered the qualities of the great planters: here was a class of selfless leaders, untainted with materialism, comfortable in its role, assuming god-like powers without qualm or hesitation. In the words of the adoring Reverend Murphy, the antebellum planters "never learned to weigh influences in the crude scales of number." They did "not know how to be unimportant." This, indeed, was one of the arts of this class. "It was its weakness—and its power." The planter preserved it within him through his personal code and by some mysterious alchemy. By "certain far-reaching, splendid inabilities," too, the aristocrat was also "saved from despair, from cynicism, from inaction." Furthermore, there was within his descendants "a certain ghostly sense of identity with thousands of his kind, now dead, to whom he must be true."

Surviving aristocrats embodied the elan of the old regime's elite and claimed the right to represent it in the new century. Their "credentials are accepted," Murphy proclaimed. Certainly they were exceptional men, "but the southerner who does not respect [them], who does not try to deserve praise at their hands, who does not desire to do as well in this warfare as [they] in the battles of long ago," was yet rarer.[2] Here, indeed, Murphy gave a model for heroes which might serve well in any time of uncertainty. Murphy himself learned his model well and followed its standard religiously throughout his entire life.

Murphy was born to a middling Episcopal family in the unpretentious, undeveloped town of Fort Smith, Arkansas; he was left fatherless at an early age and grew up in San Antonio, Texas. A sickly boy with a heart seriously damaged by rheumatic fever, he became bookish. At the University of the South at Sewanee, Tennessee, he made fast friends among the faculty and decided upon a clerical career. Murphy returned to Texas, served in rustic parishes, married a genteel New England girl, and impressed his superiors with his liberal, articulate theology.

He committed his "first public act" and showed his early concern with "the negro problem" when he protested the lynching of a black man in Laredo in 1893. Murphy persuaded the best white people of the town—city fathers, judges and the like—to sign a manifesto he had written, pledging law and order and setting a proper example for the poorer whites who had made up the mob. Murphy then moved on to serve the church in Ohio and in New York, where he began to set down in writing his convictions that the clergy should work for improvement of the human environment. By 1898, his fund-raising skills helped him win the rectorship of St. John's Church in Montgomery, Alabama. Murphy remained there and became involved in the South's major concerns: industrialization, education, and race. He undertook charitable projects in behalf of Montgomery's black population and pursued a part-time ministry "peculiarly adapted to their needs and aspirations." He spoke at Tuskegee, met Booker T. Washington and his northern white philanthropist friends, and adopted their industrial arts pedagogy as his own. In 1900, Murphy organized a great "race conference" in Montgomery, in which a brace of white governors, professors, and other authorities spoke on the unfolding racial settlement and the problem of violence. Murphy concurrently organized a Southern Society; it was composed of gentlemen like himself, and its purpose was continuing study and advocacy of racial "peace."[3]

In 1901 Murphy became involved in the new public education crusade and also helped spearhead the Lower South anti-child-labor movement, perceiving the two causes' close interrelationship. He was appointed as the salaried executive secretary of the Southern Education Board by his and Booker T. Washington's mutual friend, the powerful Yankee philanthropist Robert Ogden. Murphy's job was the coordination of a southernwide campaign to stimulate public interest in and support of the schools. Irene Ashby, the remarkable American Federation of Labor investigator-organizer, recruited him almost simultaneously to lobby for Alabama child labor legislation. Paralyzed in her efforts by public apathy and the weakness of organized labor in the state, Ashby sought some of the "best people" to aid her cause. Murphy became the most enthusiastic of recruits, soon taking over responsibility for the movement himself. He employed the usual hortatory sermons and letters to editors and pioneered in photographic propaganda in order to dramatize the human tragedy of child labor.

Murphy's widening circle of activities drew him to Washington and New York, where he expanded his acquaintances to include more Yankee reformers—Jane Addams, Florence Kelley, Felix Adler, and Samuel McCune Lindsay. In 1904 he suggested to them the formation of a National Child Labor Committee, which would systematically lobby and coordinate state work over all the country, but particularly in the South. At Murphy's suggestion the Committee hired

the dynamic North Carolinian, Alexander J. McKelway, as
its southern secretary. The sickly Murphy would be obliged
to terminate his own connections with the Child Labor
Committee and with the Southern Education Board in a few
short years, but social welfare reformers would be indebted
to this "gentle progressive" long after his premature death
in 1913.

Murphy perceived his generation standing at a sort of
moral and sociological armageddon. Threads of a tattered
agricultural elite remained, but the aggressive new common-
white democracy, led by such demagogues as Vardaman
and Tillman, which was brutal in its racism and paranoid in
its relations with big business, threatened to engulf the
region. On the other hand, the manufacturing nabobs, who
were brutal in their own exploitative ways, threatened to
supplant entirely the older Bourbon elite. Hapless blacks,
caught in this southern white scissors, would find no paternal
comfort from the new rulers.

Over the years, in dozens of speeches, tracts, and magazine
pieces, Murphy evolved an elaborate description of this
crisis and of a plan for the South's salvation and "ascendancy." He published two books, *The Present South* (1904)
and *The Basis of Ascendancy* (1910), and several very important shorter writings, "The Task of the Leader" (*Sewanee
Review*, 1907) having special significance. When he died
Murphy had also completed a number of chapters on a third
volume, *Issues Southern and National*. In *The Present South*
he spoke primarily to the white North, appealing for sympathy and passive cooperation and spelling out in detail the
racial and educational problems of the region. *The Basis of
Ascendancy* was an extension of the first book, addressed
more to the white South and much more an abstract, often
foggy, argument. These writings, plus several of Murphy's
other published and unpublished works, should be considered
together, because they comprise a fairly systematic philosophy and program.

A nostalgic concept of the Old South lay at the core of

Murphy's scheme. Murphy mourned the passing of a stable, planter-dominated social order, even though he was sadly reconciled to its doomed and archaic nature. Anticipating some of the professional historical writing of his time, he condemned slavery but approved its function of social control. He admired the old regime's harmonizing of authority and benevolence which he considered to reflect the best of civilization. Aristocratic whites accepted the social burden of blacks while, at the same time, the institution of slavery protected the "Anglo-Saxon" from race pollution. The aristocrat, wrote Murphy in "The Task of the Leader," "is under no illusions. He knows that the negro is not a white man, that the negro is not a white man in a darker skin. . . . But the very security of his sense of racial and social power makes him free to deal naturally and simply with the weaker human group. . . . The struggle of a lowlier people possesses for him an unfailing interest; he likes to see them try; he is sorry when they fail; he rejoices when they succeed." Like hundreds of other southern paternalists, Murphy treasured the dependent, subservient black who reminded him of the old days—days indeed older than he.

The Civil War had been a necessary catharsis which eliminated the embarrassment of slavery but, at the same time, freed the South from labor inefficiency. However, the war unleashed forces that still plagued the region. Citing historians James Ford Rhodes and William A. Dunning, Murphy gently but firmly condemned the Yankee for extending suffrage to the freedmen and attempting to establish "social equality." Murphy generously attributed this folly to well-meaning ignorance on the part of the white North. Knowledge of blacks—a barbaric people without a cultural heritage—would have shown that freedmen should have been left in the care of their "best friends," the white gentry. Following Booker Washington, Murphy contended that blacks had benefited from the "civilizing" tutelage of slavery because they had begun to learn the white man's ways, particularly his practical skills. Reconstruction interrupted the evolutionary process of black American history, removing blacks from kindly guidance and duping them with delusions of political grandeur beyond their reach. Alienated former slaveholders were often obliged to take physical action against the blacks and their radical white leaders in order to "redeem" the South from governmental corruption and the psychosis of interracial equality. In this vein Murphy was a leading southern white diplomat to Yankeedom in the second postwar generation.

Twenty-five years earlier, Atlanta's mellifluous orator and publisher, Henry W. Grady, had charmed northern audiences, beguiling many into a gracious admission of Reconstruction's "misjudgments." A champion of industrialization and southern white self-determination in finding a "place" for blacks in society, Grady had paved the way toward the emotional reunification of northern and southern whites; now, Murphy carried the day for the new historical consensus: slavery had been unfortunate; so were Reconstruction and legislated civil equality. Beyond the South, his writings received praise from the *New York Evening Post*, the *Boston Transcript*, Philadelphia, Chicago, and Cincinnati papers, and from such Yankee eminences as John Hay and Carl Schurz.[4]

However, Murphy—unlike Grady—was not an uncritical New South spokesman. Since Grady's untimely death in 1889, industrialization and the rise of white democracy had posed alarming threats to Murphy's conception of the South's moral and material well-being; his seigneurial model for leadership was in a decided eclipse. Experience in the child labor reform movement had taught him that many southern manufacturers—mainly, of course, the transplanted New Englanders—lacked a sense of paternal obligation to their laborers. The emergence of this new elite heralded a new era of selfish materialism, as the textiles and tobacco barons shouldered aside Bourbons of the old school. Murphy was hardly a Luddite, ready to repudiate the machine and its captains; indeed, he saw factories as the basis of the South's

material ascendancy and did not want to scare away entre-
preneurs. His solution lay, instead, in the *conversion* of the
new leadership to his own version of humane values—the
values of the antebellum aristocrat. Thus, he sought state
legislation to force humanity and benevolence upon the
factory system. The state government, in effect, would become the new *pater buono*, encouraging enterprise and
benevolence from beyond the veil and emerging to slap a
wrist only when manufacturers lost sight of the standards
of the Old South.

Murphy also accepted the inevitability of a major political
role for poor whites. Agricultural depression, the rise of big
business, and the continued struggle between whites for the
Negro vote had led earlier to the agrarian revolt—to a new
indignation and activism among the white masses. These
masses had often initiated Jim Crow legislation and black
disfranchisement; they were the racial extremists, the
"negro-baiters," the lynchers. Beginning in 1890 in Mississippi, they had had their way. The aristocrats had agreed,
for their own purposes, to white unity and the "counting
out" of blacks. The result of this agreement was supposed
to have been the pacification of the troubled South, an end
to electoral fraud, and a final solution to the "Negro question." Murphy shared with other whites a belief that racial
peace and social reform were possible only with the removal
of blacks from politics. He approved the Mississippi Plan.
Yet, this "final solution" had not brought peace and safety,
by the first decade of the twentieth century, despite a decline in the lynching rate. Dixie demagogues such as Vardaman, Tillman, Blease, and Watson perpetuated the brutality
of the Populist era, keeping alive the bogus issue of "Negro
domination," and fanning the savage flames of class an-
tagonism.

Murphy feared the masses and their rustic leaders even
more than the manufacturers. If the Vardamans lived in
terror of the lascivious *bête noir*, Murphy betrayed his own
personal horror of the rednecks: "a white population which

has not . . . the qualities of a gentle culture, which has never known the negro at his best, and which is tasting for the first time the intoxications of industrial and political ascendancy." The white masses represented brutish mobocracy in a land where a fading aristocracy and *noblesse oblige* were the only hope for salvation. It was the poor farmers who had coined "Bourbon"—an epithet describing rich men who "despised the people." Tillman, Vardaman and company represented all Murphy dreaded: war on gentility and on a helpless "backward race." Murphy feared socioeconomic leveling, but he also sought accommodation with and conversion of the masses.

Murphy set forth his plan—a marvel of hope, näiveté, and humanitarian sentiment—in *The Basis of Ascendancy*. Murphy first reviewed his version of southern history, maintaining that while "our negro population" has suffered much . . . it has received more." Blacks were "involved so inextricably in the fate of a far more efficient social group that the conditions of progress within this stronger group have become the conditions which must surround and advance the life and fortunes of the weaker." The races shared a history and a future; as procrustean bedfellows they had to make the most of it. Nevertheless, the determination of ascendancy, or downfall, still rested—as it always had—with the "stronger race."

The white man's essential difficulty lay in restraining his "instinctive revulsion" for blacks. This God-implanted feature, "the hidden and intimate hand of our society itself," had maintained race purity and control. Yet, when ignorant or evil men assailed "our fundamental institutions," as in Reconstruction, "we moved impulsively," sometimes violently. This was, as Murphy entitled a chapter, "The Protest of Our Self-Protection." Murphy approved the ends of such "protest" but abhorred the physical repression of blacks. His object was simply the maintenance of civility and decorum in a white supremacist society. Murphy's task was to persuade the white masses that benign methods were better than brutality and to reassure them that the blacks' own interests lay in white supremacy and segregation. Nearly half of *The Basis of Ascendancy* was devoted to these goals.

Murphy asserted that brutalization of the blacks was as much a practical evil as a moral one. Terror and intimidation undid racial progress and turned blacks back toward the barbarity of their origins. Repressed Negroes would become a criminal mass within society, a social albatross pulling down and ultimately drowning the whole body politic. He prescribed separate and special educational opportunity instead of brutality. Using Booker Washington's Tuskegee as a model, Murphy urged that blacks be taught "industrial" efficiency rather than political leadership. Unlike most of his white contemporaries, Murphy seemed sincere in arguing for true equality in state expenditures and in opposing valiantly those who proposed division of education tax dollars by race. Treading on dangerous grounds for a white man, he declared that "white" tax wealth was largely based upon black labor and black tenant rents and, thus, a real sharing of revenues was equitable.

In all likelihood, Murphy's liberality on the question of funding black schools was based upon his generous sense of justice, as well as his desire to see the "best" white people govern the Negroes' destiny: "The practical withdrawal of Southern revenue from negro schools," he wrote very frankly, "will necessarily mean the withdrawal of Southern influence from these schools. The State cannot abandon the education of the negro and at the same time continue to guide or control his education."

Thus, black "ascendancy" and white "race security" would be built upon white-imposed segregation, sympathetic white guidance, and the carefully managed education of blacks in practical skills. Murphy's argumentative denouement follows from this: safe industrial education ·would open economic horizons for formerly unskilled and despondent black laborers. Economic ascendancy would lead to a strengthening of the home and family. (Murphy was particularly concerned about the promiscuity of some black women.) Christian morality, a lower crime rate, the ethic of fulfilling work—in brief, a healthy new spirit and prospect—would flow from strengthened homes. The black man's own "closer identification with the consciousness and the fortunes of his race" would finally emerge from this. "It is inevitable that as he becomes more of a man he will become more of a negro." As black race confidence increased, all blacks would come to see the advantage of segregation. Somehow, Murphy seemed to believe, blacks would develop an exclusive race pride despite their continued second class citizenship and degrading racial classification by ruling whites.

At any rate, Murphy argued persuasively that white and black "ascendancy" were inseparably bound together, that black educational opportunity rather than repression was the key. The alternative was an agonizing race suicide: "A defeated race does not die instantly into oblivion; it dies first (through long and tedious processes of self-perpetuation) into the life of the group prevailing; dies as its despair makes union with the sins of the strong, into the lower life of the race above it." Those who opposed opportunity—however limited—for the "child race" would undermine the security of the whole society. This argument laid the basis for Murphy's neat coup against the Vardamans: White demagogues were principal "fomenters of the [black] race's despair." Thus, the "promoters of racial fusion," the real "apostles of amalgamation"—however "unwitting"—were "no longer the Abolitionists of the East, but those anti-negro extremists . . . who in their own war upon the opportunities of this weaker race would put the foundations of its integrity upon the shifting and dissolving basis of its self-contempt."[5]

"The fate of the strong," indeed the compelling necessity of the strong, was to adapt a paternal generosity to the twentieth century, using the resources of government only to insure that broad social needs were adequately satisfied.

The alternative was Negro demoralization, increased miscegenation, white demoralization, then ruin—an agonizing end to history.

Murphy's plan for southern ascendancy also included ultimate freedom from sectionalist constraints. Like Henry Grady before him, Murphy spoke of transcending provincialism and Civil War hobgoblins and "securing a lodgement for the contention that the Southern man has a right to make a national alliance and to associate himself with great national forces." International praise of his published writings, his many northern friendships, and especially his position on the National Child Labor Committee along with other southern whites—indicated considerable success on the part of the Alabama reformer. However, the emergence of the famous Beveridge federal child labor bill in 1906-1908 profoundly compromised Murphy's pretentions to a national role.

Late in 1906, Indiana Republican Senator Albert J. Beveridge proposed national legislation which would outlaw interstate commerce in goods produced by children. Leading members of the National Child Labor Committee, including North Carolinian A. J. McKelway, rushed to endorse the bill. A majority of the Committee soon formally recommended favorable action and resolved to lobby vigorously for it. However, Murphy, who was ill at home in Montgomery, dissented, resigned from the Committee he had helped found, broke with McKelway, and torpedoed the bill.

Murphy based his public objections on several grounds: federal legislation might endanger state laws; there was no guarantee of enforcement efficiency; a national law would provoke local resentment—a backlash—in the South; the bill was of doubtful constitutionality. Because he was embarrassed and embittered by McKelway, whom he had helped, Murphy sought to poison the mind of the Committee's chairman, Felix Adler: "McKelway and a number of others are incurably personal in controversy, McKelway especially." Meanwhile, Murphy wrote a forceful letter to President Roosevelt, suggesting that "at least six months or a year's

time be allowed to elapse before the Beveridge Child Labor
Bill is pressed for passage." The Alabamian wanted time
to work against the bill—and time to allow his old enemies,
the textile manufacturers and the untiring state righters,
to mount their attacks. The scheme worked: Roosevelt did
not use his influence in behalf of the bill; the bill bogged
down in Congress and, by late 1907, the Child Labor
Committee itself called off the fight and tacitly admitted
defeat. Robert W. DeForest, a transplanted southerner in
New York and another Beveridge opponent, gave Murphy
major credit. Federal child labor legislation would not be
forthcoming until nearly a decade had passed—and after
Murphy was dead.

Murphy's performance during the Beveridge bill episode
requires further explanation, for his motivation ran deeper
than his official objections. He often had expressed his
"practical concern" that a federal law might "embarrass"
friends working in the states—even though, strangely enough,
McKelway, the man closest to southern state legislative
work, favored the Beveridge bill. Actually, Murphy's published dissent was at least partly a smokescreen for his state
rights scruples against federal legislation. To Murphy, the
expansion of central power threatened local initiative and
democracy itself.

Beyond the issue of child labor legislation, the potential
threat of federal action to the southern racial settlement
seems to have been of particular concern to him. In 1906-
1907, as Murphy prepared chapters for *The Basis of Ascendancy*, he wrote his rhapsody to the antebellum elite, "The
Task of the Leader" (published in 1907). In the several
years prior to the Beveridge battle, he warred with Yankee
Republicans over suffrage, the Constitution, and the South.
In 1903, he defended the new Alabama constitution with
its literacy test and demanded cessation of "unjust and
undiscriminating criticism" of the suffrage settlement. The
following year, one of a presidential election, some Republicans, fretful over the loss of thousands of black voters in the

South, proposed enforcement of the Fourteenth Amendment section which authorized reduction of a state's congressional representation proportionate to the numbers unjustly disfranchised. Murphy responded in the *North American Review*: The alternative to voting restrictions would be rule by the lowest elements of both races—a nightmarish return to Reconstruction. He denied widespread discrimination against blacks, admitting only a few exceptions who had ready access to just state appeals courts. No southern constitution employed the term "negro," he reminded Yankees. However, Murphy's main point was the danger to southern blacks posed by "well-meaning" Yankees who threatened to enforce the Fourteenth—or the Fifteenth—Amendment. Such threats of federal interference in the South provoked inevitable white preemptive action which injured "worthy colored men" who had qualified under state constitutional provisions; once more, someone other than southern whites would bear the burden of guilt for southern white violence and injustice.

Thus, the gentle, facile mind of Edgar Gardner Murphy was ever drawn back to the issue of race, particularly as it figured in his grandiose scheme for a rich southern future. Federal interference of virtually any sort would upset the gains in confidence (of "race integrity") and self-determination southern whites had made since they had imposed disfranchisement and segregation. It stood to reason that the blacks would benefit from the whites' feeling of security.

Murphy was probably the most brilliant and sensitive of the southern humanitarian reformers. He had many spiritual ancestors and contemporaries, from antebellum Bible and tract proselytizers to Theodore Roosevelt and other northern patricians who hoped to quash anarchism and socialism through moderate, controlled change. Yet, Murphy's practicality hinged upon an inflexible base; his naive conception of the southern past, his faith in disinterested aristocracy, the racial arrogance he shared with his generation. The resultant philosophy and program frequently belied his essential gentility and compassion. Murphy approved of the

great race settlement with all its inflammatory rhetoric and
violence because it united whites of all classes. Only such
unity would pave the way to a new social order based upon
public education and humane industrial progress. In the
new order all whites, including veteran Negro-baiters, would
adopt a benign paternalism toward blacks. Yet in the meantime he seemed to ignore charges by some Populists—like
young Tom Watson—and labor leaders that southern political
and industrial leaders nurtured racial animosities for personal
profit and in order to preserve the division of poor white
and poor black. Murphy usually pretended that the 1890s
race settlement *really* had brought peace and that lynching
and repression had ended. He knew very well that the
white South sanctioned continued racial oppression and,
even while he lambasted the Dixie demagogues, Murphy
reserved his most impassioned condemnation for liberal
Yankees such as Oswald Garrison Villard, grandson of the
Boston abolitionist and editor of the *New York Evening
Post*. According to Murphy, "censorious and intemperate
criticism from the North"—not southern avengers—bore the
ultimate responsibility for oppression. The Yankee's duty,
like the blacks', was to stand and wait: "How long?" he
once asked, rhetorically. "For seven years?—I say for seventy
times seven years. We, in America, are dealing with no
neighborhood quarrel. We are dealing with the historic
forces of a whole civilization." A problem of such monumentality demanded a *great* deal of time, indeed.[6]

Yet, to Murphy's credit, he also demanded a great deal
of himself. Few whites in his age could claim his sincerity,
his compassion, or rival his ingenious drive to harness the
historic racial feeling of the South for humane ends.

❀   ❀   ❀   ❀   ❀   ❀   ❀

Alexander Jeffrey McKelway (1866-1918) was slightly
older, less brilliant, more flexible, in better health and

more vigorous, and capable of greater political growth than Murphy. Born to parents of no particular distinction, McKelway was raised near Charlotte Court House, Virginia. He earned a bachelor's degree at Hampden-Sydney College, a tiny old Presbyterian school in nearby Prince Edward County. After teaching public school for a year, he entered Union Theological Seminary, from which he graduated in 1891. Now a Presbyterian preacher, he married and accepted a pulpit in Smithfield, North Carolina. Following a stint there and a tour at the Fayetteville pastorate, McKelway moved to Charlotte in 1898; here he assumed the editorship of the *Presbyterian Standard*—official organ of his church in North Carolina—which he would hold until 1905, when his child labor work would carry him beyond the state and the ministry to broader fields.[7]

McKelway was a hard-driving man whose high scruples, talents, and boundless energy drove him until he dropped dead at fifty-two in 1918. He might have been successful in any of a number of fields. Indeed, he might have become and remained a prosperous, comfortable journalist-preacher in North Carolina; here he might also have lived longer. However, his upbringing, his early contacts with child labor in Fayetteville textile mills, and his expansive, resonant personality made him an outstanding social activist among southern working theologians. He accepted a social gospel mission very early: "It is a false idea of religion" that it "is concerned only or even mainly with the other world." As early as 1898, when taking charge of the *Presbyterian Standard*, he vowed that he and the paper would become activist: "the enemy of every abuse and the advocate of every reform . . . the friend of education and of temperance and of social purity . . . a Pastor to his people in the comfort of their sorrowing and the tender care of the little ones."[8]

Charlotte lay in the heartland of the Piedmont textile manufacturing region, and here McKelway began his child labor propaganda and lobbying work, paralleling Murphy's

reform career in the Lower South. McKelway delivered
anti-child-labor sermons, wrote ringing editorials, cajoled
manufacturers personally and, like Murphy, he took "Kodak"
shots of small children at their labors, sometimes hiding
himself in bushes near a factory. Some of his photographs
published in the *Presbyterian Standard* attracted Murphy's
attention, and the two men began a correspondence in
1902. Two years later, Murphy nominated McKelway for
the job of Southern Secretary for the National Child Labor
Committee. McKelway moved to Atlanta and later to Washington; he was on his way to a remarkable career in
social welfare reform.

Although he was rural in origins, a serious Protestant,
and a prohibitionist, McKelway was essentially a muckraker in faith and technique. He firmly believed in the
promise of "science" for environmental improvement and
was a fact-finder and propagandist with the muckraker's
confidence that the system would respond to empirically
demonstrated needs: "It is only necessary that the facts
shall be carefully investigated and published," he wrote,
"for the demand to become irresistible, from the people
themselves, that an industry shall not be built upon the
basis of child labor." McKelway called himself a "humanist"
and a "sociologist," yet he was much more the practical
persuader than Murphy. He became a master lobbyist and
knew the uses and users of power. His creed was "the
patient conversion of opponents into friends, the loyal support of friends under all circumstances, and the political
punishment of enemies, not as an end in itself, but as a
means to an end."

McKelway grew with the times and with the speedy
pace of social welfare thinking in his day, far outdistancing
many of his "progressive" southern contemporaries. In 1904,
for example, he opposed the idea of federal aid to education. Like Murphy, he then feared all "national interference."
However, his work and travels for the Child Labor Committee
gave him southern and national perspectives, and McKelway

grew to favor federal legislation in social fields. He regarded the South's new self-criticism, its "awakening" to
"its social problems," as a regional drift toward a "new
note of nationalism." In 1906-1907, he supported the
Beveridge bill, despite Murphy's intransigence. In 1910, he
declared that southern leaders had become "less concerned
with states' rights than with the cure of human wrongs"
and were "beginning to believe that the National government is the only agency that can successfully contend
with the great industrial combinations of our day." The
most ardent centralizer would hardly have disagreed. Meanwhile, he lobbied for years in Washington for another
federal child labor bill, which finally was passed in 1916
as the Keating-Owen Act. He favored the Adamson Act,
establishing the eight-hour workday for railway employees,
and legislation governing the working hours of women.
By 1914, he had come to favor women's suffrage and, in
1915, he supported the concept of federal minimum wage
standards. Then, in 1916-1917, he joined with Florence
Kelley, Owen Lovejoy, Samuel McCune Lindsay—all of the
Child Labor Committee—and John Dewey in promoting a
federal aid-to-education bill. The proposed legislation, partly
drawn by McKelway himself, asked Congress for $100 mil-
lion to teach English to immigrants, to build better rural
schools, and to wipe out illiteracy in the nation. McKelway
hoped that such a law would open the way for still more
federal involvement.

Yet, if Alexander McKelway rejected Murphy's provincialism, his harsh views toward blacks were not tempered by
Murphy's compassion. To McKelway, simple undifferentiated
white supremacy was as much the cornerstone of society
as it was to the most isolated eighteenth-century rice planter.
As a young man in North Carolina he had witnessed the
rise to power of fused black Republicanism and white
Populism, and he shared the conservative whites' trauma
at the "bottom rail on top." He was a participating Democrat and eager journalistic supporter of the "revolutions"

of 1898 and 1900, during which lily white Democracy returned to power and disfranchised blacks by fraud and
violence. To McKelway the future security and progress
of North Carolina and the South rested upon the repression
of blacks. No defensive argument was too bizarre for him
to champion.

At the end of 1898, for example, he responded to northern
indignation at white rioters in Wilmington in "The North
Carolina Revolution Justified," an ˙article in *Outlook*. Militant whites had slain seven blacks and wounded thirteen
in street assaults, routed the black editor of the *Wilmington
Record*, destroyed his printing outfit, and fired the building
where the paper was published. All this was regrettable,
McKelway allowed, but not the fault of the whites. Instead,
he argued, blame properly lay with the "carpetbag" Populist-
Republican state regime which had promoted equal suffrage
to "those unfitted for its responsibilities." In Wilmington
itself blame lay with the black editor, who had responded
to white rape charges against Negro men with the suggestion
that sometimes white women encouraged these so-called
"rapes." McKelway insisted, too, that most Wilmington
blacks had become surly and impudent. The slaughtered thus
became the aggressors and their own murderers!

Eight years later, he once more defended white mob
violence, this time in the case of the 1906 Atlanta riots.
Resident McKelway had been away from the city during
the troubles and killing, but he still conducted his own
post-mortem and reported his findings to the northern public, again in *Outlook*. Following a bitter summer gubernatorial primary campaign in which candidate Hoke Smith
had whipped up white racial fears, Atlanta newspapers had
sensationally exploited several alleged assaults or attempted
assaults on white women. Hysteria gripped the population;
then, a series of incidents downtown sparked white aggression in several parts of the city. In his apologia, McKelway
blandly assured Yankees that "there was nothing in the
campaign or its results to kindle ... antipathy in the

hearts of the white people." Once more blacks, whom he characterized as "the criminal class," became the perpetrators of their own brutalization. There were benefits, however, according to McKelway: "For the first time the negroes have been impressed with the truth that the individual criminal who lays his hand upon a white woman is a menace to the mass." Tom Watson himself could have scarcely put it more succinctly.

If McKelway ever shared any of Murphy's fears that the federal government might undo the South's great race settlement, they were laid to rest early in 1913 when Woodrow Wilson and his heavily southern administration came to power. McKelway had been an ardent promoter of the Wilson candidacy, and he now found enthusiastic negrophobes like himself in high places. He petitioned Postmaster General Albert Burleson of Texas and fellow North Carolinian Josephus Daniels of the Navy Department to segregate their bureaus, remove black officeholders, and refuse black applicants for appointments. Furthermore, he made common cause with influential Dixie senators Vardaman, Tillman, and Hoke Smith.

Control of black people was a principal stepstone for McKelway's program of social welfare reform. The "Anglo-Saxon's" destiny was progress. Negroes were by racial definition "criminal" and "degenerate." Thus, all kinds of interracial propinquity, especially sexual relations, had to be prohibited in order to guarantee the white destiny. Like Murphy and countless other whites, McKelway apparently shared the centuries-old white conception of the supersensuous African, so irresistibly libidinous and attractive to whites. This perhaps explains his unnecessary and irrational repetition of racial worries, warnings, and proscriptions—years after blacks were socially and politically impotent.

With so many lascivious Africans in their midst, white men required extraordinary protection and restraint. Progressive "humanists" such as McKelway found physical re-

pression distasteful, although they condoned it in all cases
involving presumed sexual aggression by black males. McKelway preferred welfare reform, however. Here, interestingly,
race served both as a reason for reform and a useful
propaganda vehicle.

An example of this process is McKelway's prohibitionist
activities. Although a moderate imbiber himself with a taste
for wine at meals, he helped charter the North Carolina
Anti-Saloon League, pressed for a state local option law,
then campaigned to make Fayetteville dry. Moving to Charlotte, he made himself so obnoxious to the wet editor of
the *Observer* that he was bitterly libeled. In Atlanta he
joined the Georgia Anti-Saloon League's successful fight for
statewide prohibition, and drafted a history of the "Anti-
Saloon Movement in the Southern States." His motivation
throughout was largely racial: "We have a child race at the
South," he wrote, "and if drunkenness caused three-fourths
of the crimes ascribed to it, whiskey must be taken out of
the negro's hands." Of course, weak whites also needed
protection, but the prohibition movement to him was essentially "the deliberate determination of the stronger race
to forego its own personal liberty . . . for the protection of
the weaker race [and the prevention of] . . . the demoralization that follows upon racial crime."

On the subject of public education, McKelway vehemently
opposed white extremists, who opposed schools for black
children. Like Murphy, McKelway called for adequate separate schools for blacks, even if whites had to foot 95 percent of the costs. Race control was once again a key
object. Whites could stymie African degeneracy and provide
skilled laborers by a rigorous inculcation of Christian morality
and manual arts: "the education of [black] children is essential to the prosperity and the peace of the native whites
. . . [and] the strong hand of the masterful race to which we
proudly belong shall compel [them] to receive that training."

Along with other child labor and educational reformers,
McKelway was most effective in scaring white folks into

reform for racial reasons. One of his most telling successes was a 1904 collection of photographs showing black
children on their way to school while white children labored
in the mills of Charlotte. When McKelway's friend Josephus
Daniels spread them across the pages of his influential
News and Observer, the pictures sounded an apocalyptical
alarm. Only a few short years before, the white South
had invented discriminatory suffrage laws which cleverly
avoided mention of race and which had been accepted by
most Yankees and the United States Supreme Court. Essential to the justification of the race settlement was the
argument that the electorate must be "fit" and educated;
thus, the famous literacy tests which fell heavily on the
former black voter. Meanwhile in the textile manufacturing
southern Piedmont, black children were generally not employed; at the same time, the public education and philanthropic campaigns were well underway and they promised—
however mendaciously—equal opportunity for the youth of
both races. McKelway's photos presented a horrific and
paradoxical forecast: black children excluded from the mills
but included in new school systems would in a few years
qualify as electors; white youth would continue to labor in
ignorance in the factories and would not qualify as voters.
All the efforts to secure white supremacy might be undone
by southern industrial progress and the very public education upon which future material well-being depended.[10]

The way out of the dilemma was the passage of strong
child labor legislation and compulsory school attendance
laws. Only then would the future be secure—politically,
materially, racially, morally. The threatened apocalypse was
complex but readily comprehended by white philistines in
the Carolinas—particularly when explained by Alexander
McKelway, master propagandist, reformer, and engineer of
the new order.

          ❖   ❖   ❖   ❖   ❖   ❖   ❖

Murphy and McKelway were rare in the South. Their respective denominations, Episcopal and Presbyterian, were not as representative of either the whites or the blacks as were Baptists and Methodists. And ministers with such social reform commitments were quite extraordinary even among Episcopalians and Presbyterians. This is not to say, however, that southern Protestant churches were benign during the progressive years. They played a critical reform role. However, in the South, especially, the churches and their pastors remained evangelical in emphasis, orthodox in doctrine. They stressed redemption—a special quality of personal experience—rather than social activism, joyful acceptance rather than energizing discontent, personal character over a restructured social order. Murphy and McKelway were thus distinctive in seeking broader reforms than prohibition and better public schools. It was more than coincidental, perhaps, that Murphy and McKelway came from industrial areas rather than the more typical country South. On the other hand, even rural southern pastors were not completely insulated from their broader profession and the outer world; they attended their conferences, read journals and newspapers, and probably at times shared the gloom which periodically infected their urban and Yankee brethren.

Preachers' motives, like others', evade the historian. Perhaps reform most often sprang from the healthy, rational choice of mature, responsible men and women. However, a comprehensive study of southern ministers as a class would probably reveal no special pattern, no hidden status conflicts or subconscious desires, but diverse individuals behaving in a great variety of ways, acting out their traditional role of moral leadership in country communities where ministers had always guided flocks in the path of righteousness. Within this perspective, a third portrait of a preacher makes sense.

Although the masses shared his reasoning, rhetoric, and politics, he was most representative *only* in being Methodist, orthodox, and a prohibitionist. As with Murphy and McKel-

way, his racial beliefs were more implicit than dominant.
He was quietly self-assured of his race's superiority. To
him, the segregation and disfranchisement of Negroes were
adequate safeguards for whites—given, of course, the added
moral fortification of prohibition. In all other respects, James
Cannon, Jr. was a superman.[11]

Cannon was born in 1864 in Salisbury, Maryland, on the
Eastern Shore just above the Virginia line. His parents
were Confederate sympathizers who had moved to Salisbury
from Delaware, where heads of both families had been
prosperous merchants and farmers. The elder James Cannon,
a resourceful, dominating individual, operated a men's fur-
nishing business, several farms, and two canneries in Maryland. Paternal toward Negroes and a devout Methodist lay
leader, he contributed to a separate church for dependent
local blacks. In 1868, he also led a secession movement
from his white congregation when the Yankee minister
could not restrain himself from making antisouthern remarks
during his sermons. So much did the Cannons admire the
neighboring Old Dominion that they reportedly named their
daughter Virginia. Mrs. Cannon was as devout as her hus-
band and a pioneer prohibitionist. Her young son James
accompanied her on charitable missions to the Salisbury
poor of both races, where at an impressionable age he
witnessed the suffering of the families of drunkards. Lydia
Cannon frequently strode boldly into barrooms, with James
close by her skirts, and confronted the evil purveyors of
booze. She founded the local chapter of the Women's
Christian Temperance Union and in ripe old age saw her
son help make Virginia dry and then contribute to national
prohibition.

James did not make the necessary public professions
and formally join the church until the late age of seventeen,
when he was away at Randolph-Macon College. In his
autobiography Cannon provided some revealing details: "if
I ever made a profession of religion and joined the church,"
he explained, "I would certainly become a Methodist

preacher, and that I did not want to be. Nearly all the church members told me repeatedly that I ought to be a preacher, and our pastors and the visiting preachers would pat me on the head and tell me how happy I would make my father and mother if I would decide to be a preacher." Young Cannon really wanted to be a lawyer and eventually a justice of the U.S. Supreme Court. He never changed. He always tried to live up to the impossible (for most people) standards and model set by his remarkable parents. When he set out to do anything, he committed himself totally. However, an amateur psychologist had best not leap to the conclusion that Cannon was frightened, repressed, and over-controlled to the point of nervous ambivalence; all evidence belies this. Instead, available accounts—Cannon's own, his contemporaries', and a hostile biographer's—indicate that James Cannon, Jr. was self-confident almost in the extreme, a cool character free of doubt. Cannon confessed later that he was stiff and unbending; he acknowledged that, following his father's example, he too seldom expressed emotion, but he regretted this little—as a mere flaw of veneer, not of essence.

An indisputable fact is that Cannon's supreme confidence, talents, and incredible energy won over his peers, betters, and a host of lessers. At Randolph-Macon, an old Methodist college near Richmond which he entered at age sixteen, Cannon's fellow members of the Washington Literary Society and Sigma Chi elected him to nearly every office available. He also won top prizes awarded by the faculty—remarkable considering his later priggishness and his penchant for condescension and moralizing. Besides office-holding, debating, and ceaseless work, he distinguished himself in rescuing and saving fellow students from the demon rum and the wrath of the college administration. Frequently, "when a friend had gotten 'gloriously' drunk and was beyond control," he recorded, "a message was usually sent to me . . . to suppress the uproar." Cannon's own description of his suppression procedure follows: "My entry into the room always had a subduing effect upon the offender. If he was inclined, however, to be violent and refused to abate the uproar which he was making," Cannon and helpers put the miscreant "flat on his back on the floor." Then, "while others held his arms and legs, I sat on his stomach. If that was not effective, some emetic was poured down his throat." This "speedily caused an eruption from his stomach of the sour beer or other intoxicants. When all the fight had been taken out of him, I usually held his head while he got rid of all the remnants of his debauch." If the case demanded a "more lasting penitence," Cannon administered "a heavy dose of castor oil."

However one interprets such episodes, one can at least begin to appreciate the proportions of the man's personal power. He was a loner. He seemed obsessed with evildoing and power, two themes which dominate his written words. Cold and relentless, he was enormously admired, feared, and hated—often by the same people. Virginius Dabney, a younger contemporary and journalistic foe of Cannon who wrote a devastating biography, called him "one of the most extraordinary personalities of his time," "a man of colossal energy, vast shrewdness, and consummate ability," and a creature of "superhuman will." Dabney conceded that another of "his doughtiest adversaries" allowed Cannon "'the best brain in America, no one excepted'."

In his first sermon, delivered on the circuit in a poor Virginia tobacco county, Preacher Cannon drew from II Peter 3:14: "Wherefore, beloved, seeing that ye look for such things, be diligent, that ye may be found of him in peace, without spot, and blameless." In his own message he began: "Laziness is a crime. A lazy man is a thief. He steals not only from his friends . . . [but from] the community." That he practiced his own preaching was as evident to all as the truth of the Scriptures. From the country circuit he went to a pulpit in Newport News, then back to the tobacco country again. In 1894, he accepted the superintendency of a half-completed, debt-ridden Methodist school in Nottoway County—the Blackstone Female Institute. He labored nineteen and more hours per day in order to build the Institute, retire its debt, staff it and attract students. According to Dabney, Cannon grew his famous scruffy beard then, "solely because he could not spare ten minutes a day for shaving." He wore the beard for a quarter century, at a time when clean-shavenness had become the style. Meanwhile he set in the black another bankrupt Methodist institution, the Junaluska Missionary Conference in North Carolina. He edited and co-owned two sectarian newspapers in Richmond; this commitment required weekly commuting from Blackstone. In addition to all this, he joined the Anti-Saloon League of America (established in 1895), becoming a national officer in a few years. In 1901, he helped found the Virginia Anti-Saloon League, which he would personally lead to remarkable victories.

Cannon did not tire in middle age of exorcising devils both secular and sectarian. In 1905, he stoutly defended the mayor of Richmond for ordering down "risque" posters advertising a ballet; the artwork revealed too much of the feminine leg. "In our revolt from Puritanism," he wrote, "the pendulum has swung to the other extreme. [Now] we are reaping the harvest of our criminal carelessness and liberalism." Two years later, he took on sophisticated fellow clerics whose theology had become "modernistic"—that is, they had not accepted the literal truth of every part of the Bible. He subscribed to freedom of thought and speech, Cannon declared, but condoning liberal theologians who voiced doubts and criticized the Bible from the pulpit was "criminal tolerance." The word, "criminal," was a Cannon favorite.

If James Cannon was a single-minded zealot, his practical talents set him apart from the stereotypical censorious fanatic. In addition to having an iron will and blind determination, Cannon possessed the skills to bring about his goals. All his sectarian ventures—the Blackstone Female Institute and the Junaluska Missionary Conference—were successful; also his many private business enterprises—which partly accounted for the success of his church projects—turned to gold. He was his father's son. Somewhere, too, he had become a devotee to the principle of the end justifying the means. He would teach the prohibition movement to deal with even liars, imbibers, and purveyors, whose aid might be useful to the cause. These traits, Dabney's cries of hypocrisy notwithstanding, made Virginia dry and "progressive."

In Blackstone Cannon struck up a friendship with a local judge, state senator, and later governor, William Hodges Mann, which would be long and fruitful. As a stolid Presbyterian, Mann believed as firmly as Cannon in Biblical truth and in prohibition. Mann was also interested in numerous other progressive issues, most notably education. Cannon, sharing the state senator's enthusiasm for public schools, drafted with him what became known as the Mann High School Act. Passed in 1908 after a false start in the previous session, it was a major breakthrough in the education movement in Virginia, providing essential funds for poor localities.

Meanwhile, Mann, Cannon, state House Speaker Richard E. Byrd, and the Anti-Saloon League systematically undermined the saloon in the Old Dominion. Between 1902 and 1908, state local option legislation—named for Mann and Byrd—laid the basis for the drying up of rural Virginia and the driving of liquor behind primarily urban barricades. By 1909, Cannon and the League were prepared to push for a law providing statewide prohibition, thus getting at the wet cities and completing the work of their cause. Furthermore Mann, who was denied the governorship in 1905, was annointed by the Thomas S. Martin organization in 1909 as its sure-fire candidate. However, Cannon met supreme frustration in the Martin machine, for Martin and other leaders, aware of wide opposition to prohibition within the ranks of their organization, refused to make prohibition statewide and were successful in forcing Mann and the League to adhere to their traditional local option position.

Mann was elected governor over a wet insurgent candidate and took office in 1910.[12] Cannon, taking his usual place in the state senate gallery above the clock, immediately reopened the drive for a statewide prohibition enabling act. He failed in 1910, as he fully expected, but looking forward to the 1912 session, Cannon carefully laid plans and labored without ceasing among the Protestant clergy across the state. He consequently came in touch with the white masses, whom he probably understood far better than Martin and company. Nevertheless, he grasped the essential fact that only by converting the Martin organization could he succeed in establishing his new moral order. After 1911, when William A. Jones and Carter Glass failed to unseat Martin and his senatorial colleague Claude Swanson in a spectacular primary battle, the futility of alignment with insurgents was more than obvious. Antimachine Democrats were fully as divided on the dry issue as were Martin's men. Thus Cannon's task was to work on the political hierarchy, from bottom to top. By early 1912, his success with the grass roots was apparent in the prohibitionist enthusiasm of the House of Delegates. But Martin snubbed Cannon again, and the state senate, closely bound to Martin's direction, refused once more to pass a bill providing for a popular referendum on prohibition. There was deadlock; the oligarchy had not budged despite his labors.

Furious and at the end of his rope of composure, Cannon was finally able to exploit both the Virginia insurgents and the machine to his advantage. Late in 1913 and in the early days of the 1914 assembly session, independent Democrats led by state attorney general John Garland Pollard formed the Virginia Progressive Democratic League. An urgent and convincing alarm went out to Martin and his men from Richard E. Byrd, who was a dry, an "original Wilson man" like most members of the Progressive Democratic League, and also a confidant of Martin. Cannon, he revealed, was considering aligning the powerful Anti-Saloon League with the "progressives" and openly assaulting the Martin machine, should the Martin-controlled senate not pass the enabling bill that session. In' order to maintain control, Martin and his henchmen had prudently responded to popular demand before. Now, the orders went out to the state senate, which, despite several comic near-disasters, carried prohibition. Martin personally persuaded a soaking wet senator to vote dry; Congressman Henry D. Flood (Byrd's relative) cracked the whip in Richmond. On the morning of the vote—Friday February 13th—Martin men discovered that the senator representing the tying vote was at home, pathetically hung over from a drinking bout the evening before; they mercilessly carried him to the capitol. The lieutenant-governor, a debonaire Confederate veteran and well-known quaffer, broke the tie. Jubilation reigned in Richmond and other communities across the old state. Cannon was reported to have smiled. Victory in the referendum, held in September, was a foregone conclusion since Cannon had done his grass-roots work so well. He had won in the southern state most notorious for "ring rule" and one of the longest wet holdouts. A great moral victory crowned the progressive era in the commonwealth.

In 1918 Cannon became a bishop of the Methodist Episcopal Church, South. He had moved by then to the nation's capital in order to oversee the successful passage of the Eighteenth Amendment and the Volstead Act. In 1928 at the height of his powers, he led the revolt in several Democratic southern states, including Virginia, against the candidacy of Al Smith, a wet Catholic. However, his candidate for governor of Virginia, an old dry crony, lost in 1929. Soon afterward, a series of scandals broke about him, concerning flour-hoarding during the World War, stock market speculation, fraud, and woman-chasing. He was investigated by his church and by the U.S. Senate and, in 1930, Cannon became the first person in history to defy a senatorial

committee and stalk out of its proceedings. Yet, he got away
with it; the courts, the senate, and the church exonerated
him. Despite a frail childhood, early-failing eyesight, a life
of bonebreaking work, the rigors of Virginia and national
politics, and a crippling disease contracted during a trip
in the Congo—he lived almost to his eightieth birthday. He
attended and made an imprint upon a Methodist gathering
in Chicago just days before his death. Such was the stuff
of which moral absolutists and country progressives were
made.

V

HISTORY AND EDUCATION —PROGRESSIVE STYLE

*Dem wuz good ole times, marster—de bes' Sam
uver see! Dey wuz in fac'! Niggers didn' hed
nothin' 't all to do—jes' hed to 'ten to . . . what
de marster tell 'em to do. . . . Dyar warn' no
trouble nor nuttin'.*

THOMAS NELSON PAGE, "MARSE CHAN," 1884

*The period of slavery was for [blacks] . . . a time
of wonderful tutelage and preparation for civilization. No lesser race ever had such a valuable
training.*

EDWIN A. ALDERMAN, CA. 1900

*We are trying to instill into the Negro mind that
if education does not make the Negro humble,
simple, and of service to the community, then it
will not be encouraged.*

BOOKER T. WASHINGTON, CA. 1900

PPER class—if not patrician—easterners dominated historical writing in the United States before the progressive
years. They wrote eloquent, monumental histories which
usually disdained the masses and the outlying provinces
and presumed the cultural and institutional preeminence of
the East. Then, after the rise of native graduate schools
and the professionalization of historical studies during the
1880s and 1890s, a new generation—the "progressive historians"—tried to overthrow the East and its seigneurial
posture and revolutionize the nation's past. The progressive writers, who were primarily westerners and southerners
from the middle and lower-middle classes, wrought an
American history more compatible with democratic ideals
and the aspirations of the West and the South.[1]

Young Frederick Jackson Turner of Wisconsin fired the
opening shots in 1893. He informed the American Historical
Association that the western frontier, not Europe and the
East, was the focal point of American history, the source
of the American character and of the nation's democratic
institutions. Celebrating the raw hinterlands, Turner appeared to rationalize and justify the rising tide of populist
radicalism.

In the next decade, Missouri-born J. Allen Smith, a veteran
radical of the 1890s monetary debate, wrote *The Spirit
of American Government* (1907), anticipating by a half-
dozen years the basic presentation of another middle
westerner, Charles Beard, in his epochal *Economic Interpretation of the Constitution* (1913). Smith, Beard and a
host of other western-born scholars—including Carl Becker
of Iowa, James Harvey Robinson of Illinois, and Vernon L.
Parrington of Kansas—argued that American history was a
struggle between liberal-democratic (good) versus reaction-
ary-plutocratic (evil) forces. Following Turner they found
that all too often the East harbored the reactionary op-

pressors, while the great outlying provinces were the sources of leveling and reform. The Constitution itself was "a Reactionary Document" (Smith's term) which continued to protect the interests against the people. Thus, all the national past before 1900 became comprehensible and serviceable to a literate generation attempting to put down a late-nineteenth century industrial plutocracy.

Of course, the East was not silent. Rather than counterattack, its key scholars joined the new intellectual wave. E. R. A. Seligman, the Columbia economist, added an important dimension to the "new history." In his *The Economic Interpretation of History* (1902), Seligman consciously borrowed Marx's class scheme. Like other progressive historians, Seligman specifically repudiated Marx's socialist prescription for capitalism's ills. He eschewed radical solutions; rather, what appealed to him in an economic-class struggle interpretation was its theme of evolution, or progress. Seligman would have Marx without an apocalypse which would destroy him and his kind along with the wicked Establishment. Instead of institutional revolution and a final end to class struggle, progressive intellectuals preferred gradual socioeconomic amelioration through bloodless conflict. Sometime, in the dimly lit future, an ever-so-gradually accumulated "social surplus" would provide harmony and justice for all.

Southern white scholars rewrote southern history with equally revolutionary effects. Ulrich Bonnell Phillips, who published his first work in 1902, was in the vanguard of the Old South historians. His *magnum opus, American Negro Slavery*, which came out in 1918, was the first long scholarly treatise on the subject. Phillips was born in Georgia in 1877; he grew up among defeated, impoverished adults prone to exaggerated reminiscenses about the good old days before the war. As a student and fledgling scholar at the turn of the century, he observed the great race settlement in the South with approval. His works on the antebellum regime were in an important way a justification of the new order in Dixie.

Before Phillips' version captured the field, the American

image of the Old South—at least in the North and West—was
essentially the abolitionists' brutal portrait. Eastern historians, such as James Ford Rhodes (who was still writing
in the 1900s) did not cavil over what seemed to them the
overwhelming moral evil of slaveholding. The white South
had been dead wrong, and virtue had triumphed in 1865
with the northern forces. Phillips—who studied briefly with
Turner, then under William A. Dunning and John W. Burgess
at Columbia—saw it differently. Beginning with "a sympathetic understanding of plantations," which he called "my
inevitable heritage," Phillips wrote paeans to the antebellum
planter which rivaled Edgar Gardner Murphy's. The "Dominant Class of the South," he claimed, "in the piping antebellum time schooled multitudes white and black to the
acceptance of higher standards." To Phillips, plantations
were "the best schools yet invented for the mass training
. . . of backward people." The slave regime was (in, perhaps,
Phillips' most famous characterization) "a curious blend . . .
of tyranny and benevolence, of antipathy and affection."

The white South finally won the war of sentiment in the
opening years of the twentieth century. Sympathetic historians in part redeemed the slaveholder and threw open
anew the entire question of the causes of the Civil War.
Ultimately, abolitionist "fanatics" and Yankee misunder-
standing would get most of the blame for the 1861-1865
holocaust. Meanwhile, Phillips' colleagues at Wisconsin, Tulane, Yale and Michigan (where he spent most of his career)
readily capitulated to his views, as did most of the historical
profession. They rewrote American history texts, southern
style, for that style had become the way of white Americans—
North as well as South. Phillips, for all his labors in old
documents, papers, and correspondence and for all his lasting
positive contributions, served the new order extraordinarily
well.

The feature of Phillips' work which was most relevant
to the new race settlement and the progressive era was
his evocation of the racial control function of slavery. Earlier

writers had assumed from the planters' conspicuous consumption that slavery was economically profitable. Phillips, who had examined hundreds of plantation account books, maintained that this was not so. Planter opulence was based upon dangerous debt and expansion which frequently led to bust and ruin. In fact, slaveholders loathed the system and were painfully aware of its inefficiency and economic costs. But climate, topography—geographical and historical accidents—had given over to them the care of a child race, endearingly dependent and contented, but also potentially dangerous. Of course, exploitation of the black labor to produce raw materials for European and Yankee factories was an important function of slavery during the process of "schooling" for "civilization." However, the more important function of the peculiar institution was racial control. Phillips clearly perceived this and set it forth in his writing. Thus, economic return from slavery was ancillary to its utility for whites who needed to govern the lesser race.

Lewis C. Gray was a Missouri-born contemporary of Phillips, and America's preeminent agricultural economist. He did not publish his massive and influential *History of Agriculture in the Southern States to 1860* until 1933, but Gray shared many of Phillips' views and lent to them his own prestige as a scholar-teacher. Writing in 1911 of the current southern scene, he declared: *"The Problem of the Negro is the Negro"* (*italics* Gray's). "Thriftless," ignorant, and crying for white supervision, he wrote, blacks had not improved as farmers since emancipation. In the cotton belt, he observed degeneration rather than progress. "That Southern institutions are repressive" Gray readily conceded. "However," he went on, "the negro is the cause of the institutions, which in turn react upon his condition." The black man thus stood to blame for his own plight. The southern white, saddled by fate with his dark burden, was no longer fully guilty even for his lapses from *noblesse oblige.*

The impact of new historical writing on Reconstruction, a trauma of fairly recent memory to southerners, was at least as significant as the Phillips' coup on the slavery question. As Yankee Republicans abandoned their commitments to the freedmen in the 1870s, northern whites began to identify themselves more readily with southern white racial opinion. As early as 1873 James S. Pike—a disillusioned Massachusetts correspondent and a disappointed office-seeker—authored the stilted, scandal-mongering, and highly influential *The Prostrate State*, a bitter indictment of the radical Republican regime in South Carolina. In 1888, John Wallace—a black Floridian and stooge of that state's Democratic leadership—published *Carpetbag Rule in Florida*, in which he used half-truths to bolster the emerging white consensus on the era: avaricious northern radicals in Congress and in the states duped credulous blacks and humiliated honest, law-abiding whites in a regime of terror and robbery. By the end of the century, as a reconciled North and South joined to "free" Cuba—and as the federal government and the Supreme Court accepted Jim Crow and disfranchisement—even such eastern historians as James Schouler and James Ford Rhodes condemned Reconstruction policies—primarily on the grounds of "the great fact of race," as Rhodes phrased it. Enslavement had been evil; so was the enfranchisement of a "backward people." Professor Woodrow Wilson of Princeton agreed with the rest in his restrained survey, *Division and Reunion, 1829-1889*, first published in 1893.[2]

John W. Burgess and his student William A. Dunning, both of Columbia, were the deans of the new reconciliation scholarship. Burgess (1844-1931) was born to a Tennessee Whig family and fought briefly on the Union side. Afterward, he studied at Amherst and in Germany, committing himself to the gospel popular on both sides of the Atlantic that the "Teutonic peoples" were innately superior to other "races" and were destined by God to rule the world. His racial and imperialist views permeated his most influential work, *Reconstruction and the Constitution* (1902), and affected his students, including Dunning. Dunning, born to a middle class New York state family, was more restrained in his expressions of racial opinion. However, his Yankee birth and respected scholarship lent stature to his assumptions about black people and the South and helped to attract a corps of gifted southern graduate students to his famous seminar. From the turn of the century until the early 1920s, Dunning's students and like-minded scholars waded through documents and wrote exhaustive state studies of the era. Some of the histories, notably those by James W. Garner of Mississippi and C. Mildred Thompson of Georgia, were balanced, enduring accounts. Others—especially Walter L. Fleming's *Civil War and Reconstruction in Alabama* (1905) and J. G. deRoulhac Hamilton's *Reconstruction in North Carolina* (1914)—were marred by negrophobia and sectionalism. The new history of the "Dunning School" and of Phillips validated and lent the imprimatur of the Ph.D. degree and academia to the southern race settlement. It was both a cause and an effect of that settlement.

The emergence of the new history shows the impact of literature upon events. From the early 1880s, for example, the national press and popular orators had stressed sectional reconciliation, often at the expense of blacks. By the 1890s, whites in both sections could weep together over sentimental, generous recollections of wartime experiences. Yankees would read as fact the Old South stories of Thomas Nelson Page and Joel Chandler Harris. Little wonder, then, that Booker T. Washington, the master of black diplomacy, employed the new white consensus regarding slavery and Reconstruction in his important address at the 1895 Atlanta Exposition. Three years before publication of Dunning's first book, *Essays on the Civil War and Reconstruction*, and seven before Phillips's first publication and Burgess's *Reconstruction and the Constitution*, Washington spoke sentimentally of slavery as a school for civilization and described slaves as loyal and contented. He bluntly declared that Reconstruction and "the agitation of questions of social equality" were of "extremist folly." Radicals had misled

blacks "in the first years of our new life"; thus "we began
at the top instead of the bottom; . . . a seat in Congress or
the State Legislature was more sought than real estate or
industrial skill. . . ."

In 1901, Edgar Gardner Murphy related a significant vig-
nette to readers of the *Outlook*. He had "just passed, upon
the streets of Montgomery a common negro drayman who
cannot, after thirty years of the advantages of freedom,
either read or write. . . ." Yet "during the Reconstruction
period" the black man had been "a prominent member of
the Legislature of this State, and . . . in company with
numbers of humble and misguided men like himself, voted
away the properties and credits of Alabama." Murphy went
on to assert the belief commonly held then that radicals
had driven the state debt from $7 million to about $35
million between 1868 and 1875 but that the conservative
Democrats, upon resuming power, "did not repudiate the
debt." Instead, to their "lasting honor," Alabama whites
"assumed it and are discharging it. But it is hardly surprising that our white people should regard the negro not
merely as a symbol of their social humiliation, but as the
representative of administrative incompetency. The South
is thus moved by something more than race prejudice.
Unlimited enfranchisement has been tried. We are paying
the cost of that trial."

Here was the Alabama legend of Reconstruction full-blown
—and told by an amateur four years before the appearance
of Walter L. Fleming's dissertation in 1905. Fleming merely
substantiated and elaborated upon the Murphy version with
more gruesome financial details. As the revisionist historian,
Horace Mann Bond, demonstrated in 1938, the conservative
Democratic government which succeeded the radical Republicans was the source of Murphy's and Fleming's information. After campaigning on the issues of white supremacy
and radical corruption, the Democrats created an investi-
gating commission to study the Republicans' money-handling.
The commission, like recent historians, found nearly all

figures relating to the debt unreliable. Records were poorly maintained, and some were lost. However, for political reasons, the commission defined certain state endorsements of railroad construction bonds valued at $21 million as "debt," thereby inflating the financial "burden" left by the Republicans. Once their political point was made, the Democrats "scaled down" the so-called debt by eliminating the bond endorsements from their new figures. Remaining, then, was a figure of about $7 million attributable to seven years of "carpetbag" rule. However, this last point was never made clear to the public. Also, considering that the radicals inaugurated public services such as free schools, the costs of Reconstruction seem remarkably low. Fleming documented beyond question the fact that there *had* been thieves among the Republicans, both white and black. But, for the most part, their thefts were petty and the state received solid services for what were apparently moderate amounts of debt.

Nevertheless, Alabamians of the 1870s and after came to accept the debt commission's double dealing and the Democrats' campaign rhetoric. They also began to see their galling poverty as an inevitable consequence of the Negro's political power during Reconstruction days. The huge "debt" which existed—then did not exist—came to live again in myth. Democratic state governments kept taxes low—most people were very poor—and schools and other public services suffered. In the minds of men like Murphy and Fleming, the old "Republican debt" thus became the scapegoat for Alabama's troubles. It was empirical evidence for them of the cruelty and stupidity of "negro rule" and of outside interference in southern affairs.

Those who challenged such enveloping myths made little impact upon the historical profession or upon public affairs. In 1909, for example, W. E. B. DuBois read a balanced paper on Reconstruction to the American Historical Association; textbook writers and editors of anthologies generally ignored it. In 1914 John R. Lynch, a former black congressman from Mississippi, published his *Facts of Reconstruction*, a decidedly personal account which might, nevertheless, have counterbalanced the accepted white version. Instead, the prevailing views of race and Reconstruction spread upward to the graduate schools and downward to the press and public schools. Speaking in Philadelphia to the American Academy of Social and Political Sciences in 1901, George T. Winston, president of the North Carolina A & M College, told of the continuing need of white tutelage for the black "child race" in the several generations following the tragic errors of the 1860s and 1870s. About the same time, Edwin A. Alderman, educational reformer and then president of Tulane University, introduced Booker T. Washington to a black audience with rueful words, condemning "that era of crime and folly miscalled Reconstruction—I hate the evil word wherein wrong ideals got set up which victimized the negro and penalized the white; wherein it was stupidly sought to enthrone unfitness, and to set the ignorant and bad to rule the wise and the good."

Also in the first decade of the twentieth century, the North Carolina-born Baptist minister Thomas Dixon, Jr., published his blood-curdling trilogy of historical novels: *The Leopard's Spots: A Romance of the White Man's Burden—1865-1900* (1902); *The Clansman: An Historical Romance of the Ku Klux Klan* (1905); and *The Traitor: A Story of the Fall of the Invisible Empire* (1907). *The Clansman* was also dramatized nationally on the stage. In 1915, Kentucky-born movie mogul David W. Griffith made it the basis of his epic triumph, "The Birth of a Nation." More paternal southerners, such as Edgar Gardner Murphy, decried the violence of Dixon's works, but the novels and Griffith's film educated a generation about the nature of slavery, the Civil War, and Reconstruction—and rendered logical and natural the great race settlement. Even Murphy could not deny this.

The same year Murphy wrote of Reconstruction in Alabama, and while Virginia's and Alabama's constitutional

conventions were in session, the *Atlantic Monthly* presented
a series of articles on the postwar struggles. They were
written by an interesting aggregation including W. E. B.
DuBois, Woodrow Wilson, Thomas Nelson Page, and Hilary
Herbert, the Alabama novelist-politico. William A. Dunning
concluded the series with a survey of "The Undoing of
Reconstruction" from the 1870s to date. He emphasized Ku
Klux Klan terror and revolutionary tactics in the fall of
Republican state governments; he recorded the courts' nullification of civil rights legislation and the withdrawal of the
Republican party from the freedmen's cause. Dunning finally
arrived at the 1890 Mississippi Plan and carefully explained
the scheme of disfranchisement. Yet, he could not resist
moralizing at the end: "The ultimate root of the trouble in
the South had been, not the institution of slavery, but the
coexistence in one society of two races so distinct in charac-
teristics as to render coexistence impossible; that slavery
had been a modus vivendi through which social life was
possible; and that, after its disappearance, its place must
be taken by some set of conditions which, if more humane
and beneficent in accidents, must in essence express the
same fact of racial inequality." Here was, of course, precisely what the southern racial reformers had in mind.
Dunning went further, however, and applied his historical
lesson to the new American empire in the Pacific and
Caribbean, where Yankees had just acquired dominion over
nonwhite peoples and then denied them equal citizenship
in the Republic. He felt that "the questions . . . raised by
our lately established relations with other races" validated
the southern racial settlement; and "it seems most im-
probable that the historian will soon, or ever, have to record
a reversal of the conditions [of inequality] which this
process has established."

The historians played a reform role sometimes through
political activism as well as through historical literature.
Woodrow Wilson as president presided over the segregating
of the federal bureaucracy. Professor J. G. deRoulhac Hamil-

ton of the University of North Carolina became an active
politician. An early convert to prohibition, he campaigned
to make his home town of Hillsboro dry; then he supported
the statewide campaign in 1907-1908. In 1912, he organized
the Wilson College Men's League in Chapel Hill and attended
the state Democratic convention as a representative from
Orange County. Two years later, as his study of Reconstruction in North Carolina was being printed, Hamilton participated in the insurgent Progressive Democratic Convention.
Hamilton, who was sincerely interested in numerous reforms,
nevertheless made the convention a sort of advertisement
for his book; he announced that drastic lawful changes
were needed to right the "corrupt" state constitution of
1868. His claim was entirely consistent with the prevailing
reform ideology.

In the final analysis, Hamilton would have agreed that
schooling was the key to the maintenance of the new white
democracy. Education was to be the reformed order's solid
guarantee to poor whites of their future ascendancy. To
neoaristocrats such as Edgar Gardner Murphy and Edwin A.
Alderman, education also would mean the salvation and
refinement of the white masses from passion and brutality.
It became a problem of diplomacy and bookkeeping to make
sure that blacks did not share equally in the educational
surge, while pretending that they did.

The creation of good schools for the masses in a poor
region was a monumental undertaking. The skeletal educational programs founded during Reconstruction languished
in the fiscal penury that followed. In 1900, many school
districts existed on paper alone, with few school houses,
few regular teachers, and terms of only three months.
Finances came from starved state "literary funds," and
state superintendencies and other bureaucratic posts were,
as in North Carolina, often sinecures held by incompetents
hostile to change. Many rural parents opposed lengthened
terms which might interfere with children helping in farm
work, and mill owners and parents of child laborers opposed

compulsory school attendance because it would remove young breadwinners from the spindles and looms, thereby reducing family income and raising owners' labor costs. Regimes representing insurgent farmers and laborers in several states increased appropriations for education and improved white schools somewhat during the 1890s but, for the most part, the Southland remained the home of the illiterate American in 1900.

Meanwhile, some determined young southern whites, seemingly oblivious to the obstacles, set out to make the common school common. In 1889, two North Carolinians, Edwin A. Alderman and Charles D. McIver, contracted with the state to conduct institutes for teachers in all of the state's one hundred counties. On each Saturday, they called public rallies to promote local enthusiasm and a willingness to bear taxation for schools. Alderman, a dapper, handsome fellow, was an especially electrifying speaker. In 1892, McIver became president of the new state normal and industrial school for white women at Greensboro; he hired Alderman as a professor, and the two continued their campaigns together. In another three years, Alderman was president of the University of North Carolina. He and McIver appeared together before legislative committees to lobby for their colleges and for common schools. Universities and normal schools would expand the corps of competent teachers; then the movement to raise taxes locally and build "a schoolhouse a day" would flourish into a genuine public school system. By the turn of the century, the North Carolina style of agitation appeared in other states and attracted the attention of southern regional reformers and benevolent Yankees.[3]

The Southern Education Board had its beginnings in the Conference for Education in the South, which began in 1898 in Capon Springs, West Virginia. Here gathered the New York-based directorate of northern philanthropy to black "industrial" schools: the financier and Wanamaker store manager Robert C. Ogden became president of the

board; members of the board included the famed financier,
George Foster Peabody, and the railroader William H. Baldwin, Jr. They were joined by transplanted southerners: Jabez
L. M. Curry, an aged educational uplifter originally from
Alabama; and Walter Hines Page, the North Carolina-born
publisher who in 1897 had delivered the famous address,
"The Forgotten Man," on the plight of the southern illiterate masses. Curry and Page subscribed to the paternalism
of their fellow members and, as diplomats to the suspicious
white South, promoted the expansion of the board to include other white southerners—Alderman; McIver; Charles
W. Dabney, another dynamic Carolina school man who had
become president of the University of Tennessee; and
Edgar Gardner Murphy, whose 1900 race conference had
attracted the admiration of Ogden and company. Booker
T. Washington was "agent for Negroes." However, even
though Ogden desired his presence at Board meetings, he
was excluded. Southern whites were already assuming control and changing the direction of a long black-oriented
northern philanthropy.

The Southern Educational Board's goal was a regional
version of the Alderman-McIver sort of educational evangel-
ism. The board would promote and propagandize. The first
educational conference in the southern heartland got underway in 1901 in Winston-Salem, North Carolina. It was
greeted by Governor Charles B. Aycock, fresh from his electoral victory the previous year on a platform which linked
black disfranchisement and "universal education." At this
conference, Aycock and fellow southerners on the Southern
Educational Board worked out with the Yankee money men
the fundamental compromises which made the educational
crusade workable in a climate of extreme racial tension.
From the southern viewpoint, the beauty of the intersectional
gentlemen's agreement was that it did not seriously challenge
the status quo. Indeed, the schools campaign would insure
the security of the recent race settlement.

Aycock and other "educational governors" shrewdly spoke for equal educational opportunity and steadfastly opposed a racial division at the state level of educational taxes, despite widespread white opposition to educating blacks with "white money." Aycock and Southern Education Board members knew very well the element of fraud in the entire issue: open division of taxes by race on the state level would invite court challenges and lengthy, costly, counterproductive litigation. The new direction of public school finance and control was toward the locality and away from the state capitol. If state legislation simply left to local administrative discretion the matter of apportioning available funds—whatever the funds' source, the whites in control would see that white schools received the lion's share.

Here was the basic arrangement for the "advancement" of southern education—an advancement primarily for whites which, while not neglecting entirely the colored common school, institutionalized educational inequality long before World War I. The Southern Educational Board agreed that, for a few years at least, they "would not emphasize the *negro* too much" (Dabney's words). *Outlook* editor Lyman Abbott, a guest of Baldwin, returned home to announce that "we have to get rid of our more or less vague idea that all men are created free and equal." After several years, Peabody suggested a campaign for black schools, but Alderman prevailed, warning against "touching a sore tooth"; finally, they all agreed that pressing for Negro schools would endanger the program for white education. In North Carolina, Aycock's superintendent of public instruction admitted that, in 1905, the state spent less money on black education than a decade before, and, by 1915, in South Carolina, the ratio of expenditures for the schooling of white and black children was about $12.37 to $1—or less equal than in 1900.

To their credit, Aycock and the southern white reformers vigorously fought attempts to destroy the black schools outright, and they despised James K. Vardaman and similar leaders for inflaming white extremism and frightening the North. Their middle way—the way of appeasing Yankees with rhetoric, while maintaining local control at home—was preferable. The Yankees merely took to heart Kipling's "White Man's Burden" (to whose stanzas Ogden would intone "Amen," even when blacks were present), a warm sentiment which was little different from southern paternalism. Best of all these Yankees were safe: they accepted disfranchisement and segregation and promoted the Armstrong-Washington style of education for blacks. Baldwin, trustee and patron to black schools, held that blacks "will willingly fill the more menial positions, and do the heavy work, at less wages" and that whites would perform "the more expert work." A North Carolina agricultural editor's defense of Ogden and his associates reveals the mood of cooperation between northern and southern reformers: "Nothing is made clearer than that these Northern philanthropists realize that the southern white man must work out without interference the South's peculiar problems and that the Southern white people are to be trusted in this work." Self-determination had finally arrived; the Yankees had now turned over money and policymaking to reliable southern whites. "They can be trusted," wrote the editor, clinching his case. By 1907, Harvard president Charles W. Eliot, speaking to Boston's Twentieth Century Club within earshot of Garrison's ghost, declared that "if the numbers of whites and blacks were more nearly equal [in Boston] we might feel like segregating the one from the other in our own schools."

Within the South, the clever educational reformers, who so successfully courted the rich Yankee and put down the native demagogue, had twin goals: the regeneration of the southern white masses from poverty and ignorance, and the control of blacks. Socioeconomic mastery of the "backward race in our midst" crops up time and again in the correspondence and utterances of the white uplifters. Charles W. Dabney—a brilliant, diligent exhorter of the white masses and director of the Southern Education Board's propaganda bureau in Knoxville, Tennessee—was as preoccupied with maintaining controlling direction over black destinies as he was in wiping out white illiteracy. The same concern underlay the work of Charles L. Coon, sometime superintendent of North Carolina city school systems and another Southern Educational Board information chief. Coon was the most rugged of fighters against school tax division and brought down a storm of complaints on himself in 1909 when he took white Georgians to task for exaggerating their contributions to black schools. However, even this generosity appeared in the context of the White Man's Burden: in return for support blacks must accept white control of their schools.

Edgar Gardner Murphy laid bare the progressive rationale with his usual honesty: "The practical withdrawal of Southern [white] revenue from negro schools will necessarily mean the withdrawal of Southern influence from these schools. The State cannot abandon the education of the negro and at the same time continue to guide or control his education." Alderman was even blunter in a Carnegie Hall speech in 1908: "It has been settled that the negro[,] having humanity, personality, economic value, shall be trained for citizenship . . . and that the [white] South itself shall exert intelligent and determining influence upon the character of that training." "Extraneous influence," he warned, "may carry the negro farther from understanding and sympathy with his environment."

Alderman, if only because of his full-time, life-long career in education, was probably a better exemplar than Murphy of educational progressivism. A city-bred man, Alderman sought to use science and technology to redeem the South; yet, as a sensitive romantic like Murphy, he wanted to preserve the superior human qualities of disinterestedness and selfless statesmanship which he felt were embodied in the Old South. "Our real problem," he once wrote, "is to try to industrialize our society, without commercializing its soul." Alderman wondered "if the thing is possible." He also shared Murphy's concern with the preservation of order, the maintenance of white supremacy, and the checking of all kinds of poor-white democracy and radicalism. Retreating headlong from Jeffersonian thought, Alderman (always the phrasemaker) declared that "freedom is a conquest, not a bequest." In 1908, he wrote his friend Walter Hines Page that he would probably vote for William H. Taft for the presidency—against Bryan and the agrarian tradition. Several years before he had clipped and preserved in his files a *Literary Digest* cartoon which probably well captured his own sentiments. The cartoonist, promoting the regulation of big business, portrayed a crude, apelike "Sampson"—labelled "The Trust"—pulling at the stone pillar of "Competition." Above, supported by the pillar and in danger of crashing down should Sampson pull too hard, was the fearful lintel, "Socialism."

Alderman had a self-conscious sense of mission for his generation, which was as acute as Murphy's. Alderman, the curriculum specialist, was interested in history and knew of late-nineteenth century developments in that craft. "History is becoming a science," he said in 1886; "objectivity" and the search for cold, hard facts were leading to the discovery of historical "principles" and indisputable laws. Soon it would not be "possible for any future Napoleon to call history *a fantastic lie*." By the first decade of the new century, he had evolved a set of truths and an articulate version of the recent southern past, which approximated the U. B. Phillips-Dunning School histories and which delineated the progressives' challenge.

According to Alderman, the South paid, until 1865, the price of industrial retardation and a quasi-feudal frame of mind because they enslaved the inefficient blacks. After the war, whites faced the dual problem of preserving white supremacy in the face of foolish Yankee radicalism and, at the same time, learning the North's efficient ways. The struggle was more or less resolved by 1900. The Yankee had been educated, neutralized, or won over; blacks were disfranchised and segregated, and a southern industrial revolution was well underway. "Here," then, was "a new world about to be born," a pivotal point in southern history.

The problem of Alderman, and of so many in his generation, was one of synthesizing opposites—the old and the new. He told an audience at the 1907 Jamestown Exposition that "an ancient, forceful and unique civilization, bred into the bone of the people, is going down before the strenuous influences of invention and modernism. Whether there shall issue something really better than the old, blending its lovableness and charm with the vigor and freedom of the new is the task set for this generation of Southern manhood."

Alderman's model New South man, quite similar to Edgar Murphy's, would somehow eschew materialism: "The Northern type—the breezy, aggressive, accumulative yankeeized Southerner will not stand the test." Like Murphy's hero, he would possess "something high, precious and distinctive in manhood and leadership to contribute to American civilization." Not unlike one of U. B. Phillips's antebellum planters, the New South man would care for the black children of all ages and "have sympathy with the blundering masses."

The historians and educational reformers were a productive combination in these years. Aiding one another, both consciously and unconsciously, they created a useful and reassuring past.

VI

THE SOUTH, THE WORLD, AND THE QUEST FOR RURAL SEGREGATION

The tremendous [racial] problem presented by the Southern States of America and the likelihood that similar problems will have to be solved . . . in South Africa and the Philippine Isles—bid us ask, what should be the duty and the policy of a dominant race . . . ?

LORD BRYCE, 1902

We would like to see the negroes of the South . . . [live] in colonies of their own.

CLARENCE POE, 1913

AS Americans quested for the Gilded Age dollar and southerners prepared for their great race settlement, a bantam dynamo named Harry H. Johnston crossed the Zambesi and conquered the shores of Lake Nyasa, thus opening the way for the addition of East Africa to the British empire. Brilliant little Sir Harry cut a bizarre figure: leading Sikh troops from India to occupy black tribal lands, the European wore a straw boater (in lieu of the stereotyped imperialist's pith helmet) with a tricolored band—black, yellow, and white —symbolizing racial harmony! Johnston—a remarkable soldier, colonial administrator, botanist, zoologist, philologist, and author—symbolized both the smug arrogance of the "Anglo-Saxon" at the turn of the century and his obsessive curiosity about all nonwhite peoples.[1]

When Johnston first entered Africa as a young man he shared the late-nineteenth century racial notions of his white contemporaries on both sides of the Atlantic. "Race" itself was narrowly construed as "stock" within skin-color categories. So-called Anglo-Saxons—Englishmen, Germans, the Dutch, probably Scandinavians but not, presumably, the French—constituted a race. Johnston and many others believed that all the separate races were "evolving" or undergoing a sort of Darwinian progress—except, perhaps, the blacks. Functionally, their evolution was almost static; at best—thought some cynics—blacks might improve to the extent of becoming better customers for cheap European manufactured articles. As the years passed, however, Johnston studied African culture, wrote of it with learning and admiration (he was the pioneer European student of the Bantu language group), and gradually altered his views on blacks. By the beginning of the new century, Johnston was out of government and cloistered in England; he had decided to include Africans among the evolving peoples.

After living and traveling throughout Africa, and writing the history of Uganda and of Liberia (among dozens of other books), Johnston resolved in 1907-1908 to visit the New World and study black people in the southeastern United States, the Caribbean, and South America. He was especially interested in white racial attitudes, the blacks' retention of African culture, and their degree of adaptation to western, industrial life. Laying plans carefully for his tour, he corresponded with and secured invitations from President Roosevelt, scholar-ambassador James Bryce, and Edgar Gardner Murphy.

Sir Harry found an engaging host and a kindred soul in

Theodore Roosevelt, who was then planning his famous 1909 East African safari. Like Johnston, Roosevelt could range knowledgeably from exotic botany to the history of the Grand Duchy of Muscovy. In addition, Roosevelt was also vitally interested in races and in Johnston's project. In letters to Johnston prior to his arrival in Washington, the president revealed his interest in African cultures, U.S. race relations, and the Caribbean, particularly Haiti. He promised to introduce Johnston to Booker T. Washington, prophesied that Johnston would find the treatment of nonwhites better in Latin America than in the United States, but averred that "at Johannesburg and Kimberley the Negroes are certainly treated worse—forced to walk in the middle of the street, and so forth." Roosevelt, very much like Johnston, believed in the destined world mastery of the Anglo-Saxon. He subscribed to the current eugenics fetish, and like many Yankee progressives declared his belief "in granting to Negroes and all races the largest amount of self-government which they can exercise." However, he confessed his "impatient contempt for the ridiculous theorists who wish to give to the utterly undeveloped races a degree of self-government which only the very highest have been able to exercise with advantage."

During his Washington stay Johnston made a trip down to Hampton, Virginia to visit Hampton Institute, which the late Yankee reformer, General Samuel Chapman Armstrong, had founded for the training of undeveloped colored people. Johnston and other Europeans had long known of Hampton Institute and Tuskegee, its daughter school in Alabama. He marveled to witness at Hampton what he had heard: that skilled teachers transferred semiliterate country blacks and American Indians into useful, adjusted people with industrial and agricultural know-how. Johnston wrote that Armstrong, the inventor of the "industrial" scheme of education, was a giant benefactor of the modern world, "a foretaste perhaps of a type of more perfected human being that may exist all the world over at the close of the twentieth century."

Finally Johnston and his other hosts, Ambassador and Mrs. James Bryce, entrained for the Lower South. They traveled to Atlanta, Tuskegee, and Birmingham in Robert C. Ogden's opulent private car. Johnston met Booker and Mrs. Washington (he described them as an "Italian" and a pretty "octaroon"), and Dr. George Washington Carver; he studied Tuskegee, toured the countryside, and watched black steelworkers at their labors. After taking profuse notes, he thanked his hosts, continued his tour into Latin America, and returned to England to write a weighty and amazing volume.

Upon his arrival in Washington, doughty imperialist Johnston had appeared to subscribe to many Americans' more inflexible racial views. With the appearance of *The Negro in the New World* in 1910, he showed his independence. Indeed, the American scene—in which he witnessed colorea peoples only two generations out of slavery engaged in complex agricultural and manufacturing duties which he had previously thought beyond their reach—accelerated his changing opinions. Johnston believed that the Hampton-Tuskegee type of practical education was the key (although he decried their wasteful emphasis upon religion and spiritual singing). Whites would continue to rule over nonwhites, but Negroes were capable of much faster evolution than he had reckoned before his New World tour. Johnston would eventually come to doubt the permanent technical and political superiority of the whites.

Meanwhile, the heresies in his *Negro in the New World* were adequate to earn the book and its author an indignant silence from America. Recognizing, for example, "the farcial side of the colour question in the States," Johnston observed "that at least a considerable proportion of the 'coloured people' are almost white-skinned and belong in the preponderance of their descent and in their mental associations to the white race." He was impressed by the apparent extent of miscegenation, and he frequently remarked upon the beauty of mulattoes and other mixed-bloods. He was so taken at Hampton by the features and coloring of a half-Caucasian half-"Amerindian" that he pondered the origins of a future race with esthetic enthusiasm. He was entirely innocent of Roosevelt's, Murphy's, and other white Americans' fears of "race suicide" and race "deterioration."

Johnston's version of American history was equally at variance with the style of the times. He anticipated the conclusions of mid-century scholars by using old slave codes and other evidence regarding the governance and treatment of slaves in the New World. Johnston attacked the then-prevalent Anglo-American view that enslavement by English-speaking peoples had been humane and preferable to enslavement by Latins: he found that the Spanish were the most humane of slaveholders, with the Portuguese next, then the French, and finally the Dutch. English-American slavery was worst of all because the law provided few institutional checks against a master's overwhelming power over his slaves. He wrote that the southern aristocracy "governed the South . . . to [the] one sole purpose of upholding the filthy tyranny of their slave system. They permitted no free press, no free pulpit, no free politics."

To Johnston, the Civil War was an unfortunate but necessary ordeal. Reconstruction was a vast disappointment—but hardly for the reasons held by Murphy, McKelway, and the younger historians: "reconstruction" is "not yet complete, nor will it be, till the Negro and the Coloured man enjoy the same citizen's rights in the eleven seceded States as are accorded" others. "What vexes my sense of justice [here he must have trampled southern sensibilities] is to see that Brother North has stepped in and borne the greater burden of the penalty; has sent his clever sons to construct or reconstruct many things . . . that he has shouldered so great a proportion of the [Union] war debt, has provided about ten million pounds sterling to educate, civilise, convert the Negro, where the very-slightly-repentant South has (in thirty years) spent barely a million."

Part of the significance of Sir Harry Johnston was that he was ignored in America, after a short-run term of intense popularity. One wonders, indeed, about Edgar Gardner Murphy's reaction to *The Negro in the New World*, as he surely must have read it in his last, bedridden years. Yet a reading of Johnston's preface might have served to counteract impressions that he was a sudden traitor to his hosts; here Johnston acknowledged his indebtedness not only to Murphy's writings, but to Ray Stannard Baker's *Following the Color Line* and to Professor W. E. B. DuBois' specialized Atlanta University publications on phases of Negro life in America. Like Murphy, Johnston was a paternalist. Johnston certainly did not share DuBois' outrage at Anglo-Saxon imperialism. Nevertheless, the Englishman's knowledge of African cultures, his detachment from the American heritage of racism (particularly the sexual fears and proscriptions), and his historical interpretations—set him apart. His work, like most of DuBois' endeavors, would wait decades for sympathetic recognition. Meanwhile, the rapidly broadening views of a scholarly old Africa hand were out of touch and virtually valueless to a United States just then adjusting to the southern race settlement and the new imperium over brown-hued overseas subjects. Johnston had departed in his scholarship and attitudes from fellow countrymen such as James Bryce, who were then accommodating themselves to the racial extremism of the Boers in the infant Union of South Africa. Sir Harry and his book were irrelevant, in fact, to a new dialogue among white men on three continents.

American interest in black Africa antedated the twentieth century. The press had riveted attention on the central African jungles during the Stanley expedition in search of Livingstone and Americans had followed the imperial exploits of subsequent Englishmen, French, and German adventurers on the "dark" continent. Meanwhile, Americans undertook religious mission work in Africa and exchanged information with Europeans about black people.

While Sir Harry Johnston marveled at the Hampton-Tuskegee model for educating "backward" peoples, American
philanthropists had similar ideas. After 1910, the Jeanes,
Carnegie, Rockefeller, and Phelps-Stokes foundations—all of
which supported black education in the South—began similar
programs in various parts of Africa. The emphasis, of course,
was upon the practical arts—especially agriculture, domestic
science, and teacher training. In the Union of South Africa
and its black satellites, missionaries instituted American
style county agent and farm demonstration work, with particular success among small freeholding Bantu. (As in the
United States there was little progress among black tenants
on white-owned farms.) Meanwhile, the Hampton-Tuskegee
idea spread up the coast of the Indian Ocean into East
Africa and flourished in Liberia and West Africa. By 1931
three-eighths of the Phelps-Stokes Fund's expenditures were
on African education and a race relations study.

By 1902, Americans from all sections had other reasons
to be interested in Africa: America's recent acquisition of
overseas possessions, the domestic race settlement, and the
coincidental occurrence of the Anglo-Boer War created a
kind of artificial world racial nexus. So momentous were
the coincidences of the new imperialism and race settlements in the United States, Latin America, the Philippines,
and South Africa that Professor DuBois was moved to declare, in the preface of his famous *Souls of Black Folk* (1903),
that "the problem of the twentieth century is the problem
of the color line."[2]

In the spring of 1898, George Dewey and his American
fleet sailed past Corregidor into Manila Bay and devastated
the Spanish flotilla, smashing a Southeast Asian empire
which had lasted since the days of Ferdinando Magellan.
On Luzon proper, a young Filipino nationalist named Emilio
Aguinaldo led insurgent forces. Aguinaldo claimed with
logic and confidence that the United States supported independence and had no imperial designs on the archipelago.
However, in the following year, the United States annexed

the Philippines and Aguinaldo again became an insurgent—
this time against different foreigners. While American troops
(ultimately tens of thousands of them) fought an undeclared
war against Asiatic guerillas, Congress and an ambivalent
American public debated the war throughout a presidential
election year.

Racial theories played a key role in the complex national
debate and were the common ground on which both imperialists and anti-imperialists stood. Those favoring annexa-
tion urged Americans to take up the White Man's Burden;
opponents argued that responsibility for yet more millions
of nonwhites would endanger Anglo-Saxon institutions and
racial purity. Neither side believed that the Filipinos could
govern themselves. In 1900, young Senator Albert J. Beveridge of Indiana, just returned from a Pacific tour, declared
that the United States "will not renounce our part in the
mission of our race, trustees under God, of the civilization
of the world." In his anti-imperialist campaign tract, *Republic
or Empire?*, William Jennings Bryan defended Jim Crow at
home while insistently condemning United States control over
a "backward race" abroad. Senator Henry Cabot Lodge,
leader of the imperialists, countered neatly: "Bryan and his
party think we should abandon the Philippines because they
are not fit for self-government. I believe that for that
very reason we should retain them."

Expressions of American naïveté, fear, and arrogance toward nonwhite foreigners abounded. Newspaper and periodical cartoonists depicted Aguinaldo and his fellow insurgents
as banjo-picking, minstrel-like Negroes, and southerner and
Yankee vied with each other in racial derogation of Filipinos. Samuel Gompers wondered "what is to prevent the
Chinese, the Negritos, and the Malays [from] coming into
our country?" David Starr Jordan described the Philippines
as lying in the "torrid zone," unfit for Anglo-Saxon habita-
tion and the home of an inferior racial stock; whites would
deteriorate there. Senator John W. Daniel of Virginia, a
florid, limping Confederate veteran, described Filipinos as

"a mess of Asiatic pottage," unworthy of membership in the American family. A colleague from the state of Washington warned of "a mongrelizing [of] our citizenship . . . [a] debauching [of] our institutions . . . by an assimilating miscegenation." Benjamin R. Tillman delighted in bedeviling Yankee Republicans, especially Lodge, about their changed attitudes toward citizenship and nonwhite people since Reconstruction days. Tillman was unkind, for the white South had won a great victory; belaboring the point was unproductive. Already, as C. Vann Woodward has written, the Mississippi Plan had become the American Way. Meanwhile, writing from darkest Mississippi, Mrs. Jefferson Davis informed readers of *The Arena* that Filipinos were "negroes"—a term becoming generic for nonwhites. She believed that, since their emancipation, American blacks had drifted backward into barbaric criminality: "I cannot see why we should add several millions of negroes to our population when we already have eight millions of negroes in the United States."

The Filipino rebellion paralleled the Anglo-Boer War. Boer grievances against the British dated at least as far back as 1833, when the British had abolished slavery throughout their empire. The independent-minded Boers had thereupon trekked northward out of reach (they thought) of British do-gooders and established "free states" on the Orange River and in the Transvaal. They wanted self-determination in racial policies. Then, late in the century, gold bonanzas on the Rand brought in English capitalists and miners of many nationalities—including black and yellow ones. The Boers lost their grip on government; violent incidents and bad command decisions led to war.[3]

The British, overwhelming their adversaries with men and arms, found themselves mired in a long anti-guerilla action not unlike the Filipino-American affray on the other side of the globe. Boer generals took to the bush, and the British established concentration camps in their desperate attempts to gain control and bring the Boers to heel. World opinion favored the underdogs. Americans staged a great pro-Boer rally in New York City; speakers, who were seemingly mindless of American policy in the Pacific, compared the Afrikaaner struggle to the American War for Independence. One orator made allusions to the Boers having redeemed South Africa from "savagery and barbarism."

The struggle galvanized the Boers and fractured the British. Deep public divisions finally ripped the government; the hard repressionists gave way, and the British policy became one of magnanimity and "racial unity"—that is, unity of the two white nationalities in South Africa. Britain finally recognized peculiar local conditions and assured the Boers that the Orange-Transvaal race system would be left undisturbed. After the further agreement that the liberal Cape Colony "color blind" franchise would not be extended into the Boer states, the Boer negotiators made peace at a place appropriately called Vereeniging—Union. Thus, while Britain's military victory reaffirmed South Africa's colonial economic and political status, the Boers won what was to them the more important issue, the maintenance of their control over black natives. As in the aftermath of the American Civil War, the vanquished at arms became the victors at peace—at least so far as racial matters were concerned. This laid the foundation for the Union of South Africa, formally created in 1910, and also for the modern system of *apartheid*.

The years of the South African accommodation, American colonial expansion, and the southern racial settlement witnessed increased communications and a heightened sense of comradeship among whites on three continents. Englishmen, Boers, English South Africans, and Americans paid close attention to developments on either side of the Atlantic, read and reviewed each other's books, and took comfort in comparing each other's racial problems and solutions. In June 1902 (the year of Vereeniging), for example, James Bryce—diplomat, scholar, and the foremost foreign authority on the United States—delivered the Romanes Lecture at Oxford. His topic was "The Relations of the Advanced and the Backward Races of Mankind" and, because of his own stature and the prestige of the Romanes Lecture, Bryce fastened international attention upon the similarity of race problems around the globe: "The tremendous problem presented by the Southern States of America, and the likelihood that similar problems will have to be solved elsewhere—as, for instance, in South Africa and the Philippine Isles—bid us ask, what should be the duty and the policy of a dominant race where it cannot fuse with a backward race?" Taking his cues from the United States and from the emerging South African pattern, Bryce proposed that colored peoples "under the care" of whites be guaranteed "citizenship rights"—except that of the franchise, which might be awarded to a few "superior" blacks. (He would also disfranchise illiterate whites.) Bryce favored antimiscegenation laws and statutory physical separation of the races until such time as "good feelings" could gradually be developed. Nonwhites would ultimately enjoy full equality, although it seems fair to add that Bryce probably did not envision a time of actual social equality which included interracial marriage. He was not explicit but, in all likelihood, he—like Edgar Gardner Murphy —thought in terms of a separate-but-equal society with true justice for both races. Lord Bryce's remarks were reproduced and discussed with interest in the American press. Murphy thought Bryce's recommendations so relevant that he had a portion of the lecture reprinted as an appendix in his *Problems of the Present South.*[4]

In his *Asia and Europe* (1904), Englishman Meredith Townsend used "evidence" on American blacks to buttress his imperialist arguments about the Orient. He observed that after three hundred years, New World Negroes remained hewers of wood and drawers of water. Townsend, who was diametrically opposed to Bryce and Johnston, declared nonwhites to be innately inferior in a functional sense. The white must think, do, and rule everywhere. In the Transvaal, Orange Free State, and Natal, aggressive whites looked to the American South for segregation laws; in Mississippi planter-economist Alfred Holt Stone, a much published commentator on race in America, referred to the Transvaal and its similarity to Mississippi.

Of course, there were also vast dissimilarities between the Transvaal, Luzon, and Mississippi. Bryce, Murphy, Stone and other writers seemed aware, for example, that the Bantu and Malays were natives of their respective lands, with their own languages and long cultural traditions, that they overwhelmingly outnumbered white settlers and intruders, and that they had not been so affected by slavery as had American Negroes. Yet, at the turn of the century similarities between the American South and other bi- and multiracial societies became more important than the differences. After 1899, the experiences and racial policies of southern white men achieved a certain international relevance and received sympathetic attention they never had before. The South, at odds with Atlantic civilization in 1861 because of its peculiar racial system, found itself a respected equal—perhaps even a wise counselor—in that same world community forty years later.

This atmosphere still prevailed in 1912, when young Clarence Poe of Raleigh, North Carolina met Maurice S. Evans of Durban, Natal. Poe, editor of the *Progressive Farmer*, was passing through London during a tour of foreign agricultural systems. Evans, a merchant and politician, had been a framer of the constitution of the Union of South Africa and earned an international reputation as an authority on race relations. As the Union took shape, he wrote *Black and White in South East Africa* (1911), an influential book which argued for racial separation in order "to prevent race deterioration, to preserve race integrity, and to give to both [races] opportunity to build up and develop their race life." In 1912, Evans was promoting legislation to guarantee segregation in rural areas of South Africa (the Land Act of 1913), and he was planning a tour of the American South which would result in the publication of his much-read *Black and White in the Southeastern United States* (1916). Here Evans took note of differences between South Africa and the

American South: nevertheless, he prescribed more segregation for America, according to the emerging South African
model of separate development.

Although his meeting with Evans helped to catalyze his
grandiose vision of reform for the South, race was but one
of Clarence Poe's concerns. Clarence Poe's early life illustrates the continuity in rural American politics from populism
to Bryan-style democracy and the impact of trans-Atlantic
communications on racial matters. Reared on a farm in
Chatham County, North Carolina, Poe was the son and
nephew of Alliance yeomen who voted for James B. Weaver
in 1892. Poe early displayed a facile mind and pen; he had
been weaned on reformist literature and the homey virtues of
the Protestant countryside. At sixteen (1897), he attracted
the attention of the editor of the Farmers' Alliance organ,
the *Progressive Farmer*, who invited young Clarence to become assistant editor. Poe settled in Raleigh and assumed
full editorial duties before his nineteenth birthday. In four
more years, he owned controlling interest in the weekly
paper and, by 1910, the *Progressive Farmer* blanketed the
South, from Virginia to Texas, in five editions. In the meantime, Clarence Poe had become a progressive Democrat, a
ubiquitous reformer, and one of the most influential opinion-
molders in the South.[5]

Poe was an energetic moralist with a practically all-
encompassing social conscience. Appalled by the high ratio
of saloons to population in Raleigh, for example, he became
a prohibitionist and, with Alexander McKelway and Baptist
editor Josiah W. Bailey, he helped make North Carolina
one of the first dry states. He also campaigned successfully
for a boys reformatory, public ownership of urban utilities,
clean government, decent midway entertainment at state
fairs, and honest advertising. His passion was expanded
public education, and Poe made the *Progressive Farmer* an
unofficial organ of the Southern Education Board; at one
point, he served as an officer in the movement. By 1912,
when he helped establish the Southern Sociological Congress

at Nashville, he projected the scope of his interests to encompass the entire South. The Sociological Congress, which
was a forum for many reformist goals, served as an impetus
to the formation of similar organizations on the state level.
Poe himself founded the North Carolina Conference for Social Service and was its president from 1913 through 1915.
Under his leadership, the Conference actively promoted a
legislative reform program, most of which was realized by
1917. Although he never held public office, Poe made solid
contributions to reform in North Carolina and, through the
Progressive Farmer, Sociological Congress, and other groups,
he influenced change beyond the borders of his home state.

Despite the breadth of his activities, however, the Carolina
editor was essentially an old-fashioned agrarian, a "Jeffersonian," because he believed that the noblest virtues of
American life were nurtured on the farm. Poe, like other
spokesmen of the "New South," promoted manufacturing
and accepted the "inevitability" of urbanization; yet, much
of his urban reform effort appears to have been rooted in a
profound suspicion of cities. Poe became convinced very
early that a great moral crisis existed which might be
checked and overcome only by a strengthening of rural life.
The youth fleeing to the cities must be persuaded that
country life was preferable; farmers must find solutions
to their problems of production, credit, and marketing.
There would only be a reservoir of moral strength to buttress and sustain the virtues of individual integrity, clean
living, and religious faith when the rural sector was secure.
Sweeping innovations were in order and, in 1912 and 1913,
Poe formulated a rural reform program of unprecedented
comprehensiveness.

In the summer of 1912, Poe toured the British Isles and
the Low Countries, studying agricultural conditions and
organizations. In "backward Ireland," in England, and on
the Continent he was surprised to find a satisfactory rural
life—made so he believed, by cooperative credit societies.
Southern farmers entrapped by the crop-lien-single-staple

syndrome, might achieve economic security by adopting this European solution to the credit problem. However, Poe was far more impressed by the farm village clusters he encountered; the sight of farmers living close together came almost as a shock to one accustomed to the broad, sparsely settled spaces of the American scene. Poe returned to North Carolina deeply inspired and convinced that he had finally found the solution to the agricultural South's enduring dilemma.

Poe unveiled and expounded his vision of "a great rural civilization" in the South, between mid-1913 and 1915, in speeches in both Carolinas and Tennessee as well as in *Progressive Farmer* editorials. The scattered, individualistic, unorganized rural existence common to America was an anachronism in the modern world. Fierce economic competition among farmers led to overproduction, victimization by "trusts," and human suffering. Furthermore, rural life meant isolation and social deprivation. Poe believed that the flight from the farm was as much a quest for human "society" as for economic betterment. Possessed by his new concepts of country living, he called for a vast reorganization of southern agriculture along the lines of the European models he had observed in 1912. Paradoxically, in order to preserve rural life he would create special towns on the countryside—"rural communities," or modern rationalized villages.

Poe insisted that the population "must [be] massed for best results." Only when people lived in close proximity and in an efficient manner could they achieve affluence and a rewarding social life. Poe envisioned in his proposed communities the establishment of credit societies, community-owned banks, cooperative warehouses and marketing facilities, and convenient social halls and churches. Every inhabitant would receive a practical "education for efficiency and production." Classical learning would be subordinated to scientific agricultural training, which was directed toward "mastering environment." Much would be demanded of these modern, skilled farmers, but the rewards would be commensurate—"freedom from centers of drink, vice, and immorality" not the least among them. He implied that the creation of such efficient, Christian, and well-ordered little villages was the only alternative to spiritual—and material—decay.

Contemplating the barriers to be overcome before his vision could be realized, Poe saw one which dwarfed all others in comparison—race. For Poe, the southern country-side was not only a barren place to live; it was rapidly becoming a black man's country. Black occupancy and ownership of farms had advanced almost everywhere; between 1900 and 1910, Negroes gained a million acres over whites in the Carolinas alone, and similar situations were apparent in Georgia and Arkansas. This advance was due to "unfair competition" and "social pressure." Blacks were willing "to underlive the white man." A Negro might be a good hand on the farm, but he was not a good neighbor, particularly when too numerous. Anglo-Saxons, he wrote, instinctively repulsed by the inferior child race, fled rural neighborhoods when blacks equalled or exceeded them in numbers. Race prejudice made impossible the cooperative spirit essential to building "a great rural civilization."

Anyone acting upon Poe's premises would arrive by logic alone at the conclusion that rural areas should become racially segregated. The urban segregation movement, begun in Baltimore in 1910, was then spreading southward. However, Poe's inspiration was at least in part external in this matter, as it was in the case of the village clusters. Editorially recounting his London interview with Maurice Evans, he initiated in the *Progressive Farmer* a "South-Wide Campaign for Racial Segregation" on August 2, 1913. He planned to model a new southern rural system from the latest technology, Jeffersonian idealism, and the South African arrangement.

Poe also exploited the current "yellow peril" on the American West Coast in promoting his program for the South. In the same *Progressive Farmer* issue which recounted the Evans interview, he featured a story on California racism. There recent legislation had outlawed the ownership of land by Japanese. Poe opposed such measures, feeling that all races should have opportunity for self-development. Yet, throughout the world, "social and economic questions intermingle like warp and woof in this problem of the meeting of the races." He contended that not only white South Africans and Americans from the West and South but the editors of the *Outlook* and *Collier's Weekly* were dedicated to white supremacy. "We would like to see the negroes [of the South] own the land they till. . . . but we want to see them buy in colonies of their own." For Poe race had become the "Greatest Problem Facing Our Southern Farmers," more important even than "economical production . . . more scientific marketing . . . better rural credits . . . [and] a better educational system."

The chief vehicle for Poe's campaign, aside from the *Progressive Farmer*, was the North Carolina Farmers' Educational and Cooperative Union. First organized on a statewide basis in 1908, the Farmers' Union was at its membership peak during the years of poor cotton prices, from 1911 to 1914. The state organization's president was Dr. H. Q. Alexander, a dynamic and somewhat erratic Mecklenburg County farmer and physician. J. Zeb Green served as organizer-lecturer and editor of the Union's organ, the *Carolina Union-Farmer*. Clarence Poe was a member of the Union's executive committee. Its lobby, the State Advisory Board, of which he was also a member, met in Poe's Raleigh office. In the late spring of 1913, as the "rural civilization" campaign was about to begin, Poe absorbed the *Carolina Union-Farmer*, and the *Progressive Farmer* then became the official organ for the Union. Poe found Alexander and Green eager coworkers and, from this strengthened position, the editor began to expand his educational network.[6]

In order to further his crusade, Poe organized the North Carolina Committee on Rural Race Problems in early October 1913. The Committee's objective was to influence public opinion and legislation. Josiah W. Bailey, Raleigh lawyer, editor of the Baptist organ, the *Biblical Recorder*, and future United States Senator; former North Carolina House speaker Edward J. Justice, "Progressive of Progressives"; and General Julian S. Carr, respected businessman, reformer, and a venerable Confederate veteran were among the organizers. Poe was president; H. Q. Alexander, first vice president; J. Zeb Green, secretary. At the beginning of 1914, Poe prevailed upon the North Carolina Conference for Social Service to incorporate a rural segregation plank into its ten-part program for "social progress." Poe prepared the way for what he hoped would be a state-sweeping crusade for reform. Rural segregation would be a major part of the parcel.

Soon after the Conference's winter meeting, Poe, Bailey, and Alexander issued a "call" for a mass "progressive Democratic" convention to meet at Raleigh on April 8, 1914. The convention would agree upon a program, help elect legislators friendly to it, and generally accomplish broad reforms without revolution or social upheaval. Seven hundred delegates, many of them Farmers' Union members, attended the conclave. The progressive platform drawn up for discussion by Poe and company included tax reform, six months schools, railway rate revision, child labor and penal reform, the initiative and referendum, and rural segregation. However, here Poe met his first defeat.

Secretary of State William Jennings Bryan, idol of rural reformers, had been invited to deliver the principal address. However, hearing of the prominent segregation issue in Raleigh, (as one source relates it), Bryan contracted "a cold" and declined to come. Then, a majority of the delegates rejected Poe's pet proposal, and rural segregation was not included among the eight planks of the final convention platform.

Nevertheless Poe pressed on, apparently hoping for Farmers' Union pressure upon the forthcoming General Assembly. The 1913 legislative session had concluded too early (or Poe concocted his vision too late) for action on rural segregation that year, but he looked forward to success in the spring of 1915. In the meantime, he drafted a disarmingly simple model for the anticipated legislation: when the "greater part of the land acreage" in a rural neighborhood was owned by members of one race, "a majority of the voters" might forbid the sale of land to members of the minority race; in "consideration of the peace, protection, and social life of the community," a reviewing judge or board of county commissioners would allow or disallow each majority decision.

Poe's proposal was vague and haphazard—by design; it was looser even than the Richmond, Virginia urban segregation plan, to which it bore a resemblance. In particular there was no provision for eliminating tenants of the wrong color from respective racial districts. Poe was well aware of his glaring omissions, but feared abuses to both races in a complicated land code. He wished to implement segregation within the simplified Torrens system of land registration and, for this reason, he felt that a compelling public opinion against whites' renting or selling land to blacks must become prevalent. The editor desperately tried to generate this attitude by exhortation and personal example. The Poe family homestead in Chatham was "absolutely vacant this year [1915], we having refused to sell to a negro, and the white family who were there last year having left because there were not enough white neighbors in the community." Poe celebrated his cousin, who remained in the area: "He is a hero of the rear guard of our ancient Anglo-Saxon civilization who still keeps the colors flying and still wages a valiant battle to hold a community for the white race," although "almost surrounded by a silent, insidious, ever-advancing opposition." The cousin was representative, a "type of thousands and thousands . . . all over the South, from Virginia to Texas . . . whose appeals, alas, have been but voices in the wilderness, unheard and unregarded by the town-dwelling leaders of our race."

Poe demanded sacrifices of white southerners: they should perform all manual labor themselves and abandon black labor. "Whenever an inferior race and a superior race exist side by side, and to the inferior race is given a larger share of the manual labor, the fatal tendency is for the superior race to lose the fibre of strength and vigor that comes only through grappling with the big, rough, elemental tasks of industry." Industrious white yeomen would build the "great rural civilization" by the sweat of their brows, while blacks, spared direct competition with whites, would also benefit from segregation and develop a black "society." To large planters who depended upon extra hands, Poe promised that if rural segregation became a reality, both white and black laborers in the South (of course heeding Poe's gospel of work) would feel safe from racial competition, as would thousands of immigrants from Northern Europe.

In late 1914, the editor and his Farmers' Union colleagues decided that a state constitutional amendment would be the most effective—and repeal-proof—means of securing rural segregation. However, the usual difficulty of passing amendments and the grandiosity of Poe's plan spelled legislative defeat the following spring.

The nature of the opposition which defeated rural segregation was evident in the columns of the *Progressive Farmer*, and Poe was bitterly aware of his enemies' identities: hypocritical Democratic "town politicians" who, safely segregated in the cities, regarded the proposal as "radical"; supply merchants and bankers unwilling to refuse business and credit on a racial basis; absentee landowners reluctant to make the sacrifices which Poe demanded of himself (that is, refusing to sell or rent to blacks); and most significant, planters who preferred black to white labor because they could "manage them better." The bluntest statement of this last group was written by one W. M. Webster of Winona, Mississippi: "I have lived in the South all my life," he declared. "I have tried farming with white labor and made a failure. The white man does not take to the hoe and plow like the colored man and is more expensive." The white laborer "wants his coffee three times daily and everything else in proportion. You can tell the colored man what to do and what you want done. . . . We cannot get along without the blacks. The day that comes when they are segregated, I want to go with the negro."

Opposition also came from blacks and other southern white reformers. W. E. B. DuBois condemned the Poe plan and Booker T. Washington worked quietly against it. Dr. Charles Hillman Brough, of the University of Arkansas and president of the University Commission on Southern Race Questions, attacked the Poe scheme at a meeting in Washington in December 1914. The editor of the *Souther Planter* (Richmond, Virginia), the *Progressive Farmer*'s largest competitor in the Upper South, also discredited rural segregation, repeating a distorted white version of Washington's formula: "the white man's brains and the negro's brawn should unite in building the New South."

A most telling attack came from North Carolina, from the pen of Gilbert T. Stephenson, a Winston-Salem judge and the prestigious author of *Race Distinctions in American Law* (1910). Writing in the *South Atlantic Quarterly*, Stephenson dispensed quickly with practical and constitutional arguments and took Poe to task on "moral" grounds. He argued that rural segregation was "immoral" in that it circumvented God's sacred injunction to white men to uplift blacks by helping them and showing them the way by good example. Rural blacks, encouraged to congregate in communities all their own and left to their own devices, would develop pestholes of moral and physical depravity comparable to city black districts. Stephenson maintained that moral, benevolent whites did their duty by maintaining propinquity and socially controlling the "child race."

Poe, who had thought of himself as fatherly protector of Negroes, was sorely wounded. Responding to Stephenson in the same journal, he declared: "I hope I shall never be classed with the bitter or destructive type of 'negro agitators'. . . . If I know my own heart I would not be unjust to the negro. For the Shylocks and vultures of our own race who fatten financially upon his ignorance and weakness I have nothing but the utmost contempt and loathing. For all who would oppress him and keep him in peonage I have no shadow of sympathy.

Had Poe been less defensive-minded, he might have returned an attack upon Stephenson for certain inconsistencies and hypocrisies. In his book on the legalisms of race distinction, which was based upon his philosophy of noblesse oblige, Stephenson had forcefully approved of segregation in transportation, public accommodations, education, and urban housing. If such segregation laws did not exist, he wrote paradoxically, "the stronger race would naturally appropriate the best for itself and leave the weaker race to fare as it could." In other words, physical separation itself protected blacks from the brute superiority of whites. "The honest enforcement of race distinctions," therefore, "would be to the advantage of the weaker race." Stephenson apparently believed that what was benevolence for the town was not for the country, or he had undergone a radical change of heart in three years time.

Poe seemed particularly stung by criticisms from small black farmers within the South, some of whose bitter letters he printed in the *Progressive Farmer*. For example, a rural resident of Mississippi eloquently protested that, whatever Poe's intentions, he was stirring up racial animosity. Poe sincerely believed that he was working for racial peace and flatly disclaimed responsibility for the Mississippian's problems.

There is no doubt that Clarence Poe did wish blacks well —as long as "racial integrity" was preserved on both sides. A decade before, Poe had decried the "frenzied abuse of the negro" in Thomas Dixon's *The Leopard's Spots*; he was also a consistent foe of lynching. As an advocate of equality for black public education, he had vigorously and successfully fought a move in North Carolina to divide education taxes by race. Nevertheless, Poe was not above demagoguery. His "black peril" editorials on the advance of Negro land occupancy in 1913 no doubt aroused white fears, and, by early 1914, his campaign had descended to the inevitable miscegenation issue. In an editorial entitled "The Menace of the Mullato," Poe claimed that rural integration had produced an alarming increase in sexual "crime" since the end of slavery. (He apparently did not consider that antebellum plantations were also "integrated.") Despite Poe's usual gentlemanly restraint and his humane intentions, the black Mississippian's anger was justified.

Poe only slowly began to despair of realizing his segregated "great rural civilization." He cried for "justice to the white farmer" at the University of Virginia's 1915 commencement. In September of that year, he suggested that the South adopt a township type land system as a step toward rural segregation. Later in the fall, Poe attempted to rally his friends, but now practical men such as Josiah W. Bailey had prudently abandoned the cause. The campaign had in fact already disintegrated. Soon World War I would preempt the editor's attention and, although he never abandoned his dream of a prosperous, rewarding life for the southern farmer, black and white, no more was heard of this scheme to extend racial separation.

There was to be no "great rural civilization"—at least not until long after World War II, when cotton went west, cattle came east, and the blacks went to Washington, New York, and Chicago. While the South became the land of proliferating *de jure* segregation, its vast countryside, where the average southerner lived, had only *de facto* segregation—and in a literal sense, a great deal of integration. Presumably, there also persisted along with rural integration the same hypocritical paternalism and the same economic exploitation of Negro labor that Poe always condemned. The most ambitious of all the progressive racial reform movements had failed.

VII

PROGRESSIVE AGRICULTURE

We must . . . set in motion the benign methods of aided individualism.

WESTMORELAND DAVIS, 1909

THE best known American progressives resided in cities and belonged to the broad urban middle class. But many of them were rural in background and still idealized the independent yeoman farmer. Many urban reformers came from provincial farms and towns and carried with them the moralism of country Protestantism and the McGuffey Reader. In the cities they reacted against slums, crime, congestion, and the seemingly hopeless complexity of urban life and yearned for old virtues, simplicity, and a sense of community. "In the smaller towns and country districts," mourned a middle western editor in 1915, "people say 'we,' when they speak of governmental activity. 'We' built the courthouse and got it done at low cost." But "in the big cities people say 'they'; why don't 'they' do thus and so? . . . It isn't a personal matter with them. The government isn't their government." Ray Stannard Baker wrote of the same contrast: "My ancestors . . . had wilderness. . . . I found teeming, jostling, restless cities; I found a labyrinth of tangled communications . . . hugeness and disorder."[1]

At the turn of the century, many Americans probably possessed such concerned yet nostalgic outlooks. The nation changed rapidly under the impact of manufacturing and urbanization, and people caught in the transition sought stable reference points. Inevitably, a rural and agricultural way of life became most idyllic in the eyes of those most removed. In 1908, for example, urbanite Theodore Roosevelt undertook to "warn my countrymen that the great progress made in city life is not a full measure of our civilization; for our civilization rests at bottom on the wholesomeness, the attractiveness and the completeness, as well as the prosperity, of life in the country." Farm men and women "stand for what is fundamentally best and most needed in our American life," he wrote, and "upon the development of country life rests ultimately our ability, by methods of farming requiring the highest intelligence, to continue to feed and clothe the hungry nations; to supply the city with fresh blood, clean bodies, and clear brains that can endure the terrific strain of modern life."

Relative to this lofty sentiment, Roosevelt announced his appointment of a blue ribbon Country Life Commission. The Commission would conduct nationwide hearings in the fall of 1908 and also mine the brains of its prominent membership. Finally, it submitted suggestions to the president for the solution of rural problems. Sentimental conservationist Roosevelt, like so many of his urban contemporaries, looked to the farm as a haven of stability in a time of changing morality. The city was dependent upon the farm for salvation from iniquity; yet, paradoxically, farming had become for many an unreliable business and was losing both its bucolic charm and its young people. The city symbolized progress and moral laxity; the farm was moral yet materially retrogressive. Progressives of all sections yearned for a new rural order to rectify this double peril.

Roosevelt's Country Life Commission stood for farming both as "a way of life" and as a business. The Commission— investigative, hortatory, and impotent—was an expression of both sentimentalism and practical concern. Committeemen Liberty Hyde Bailey and Kenyon L. Butterfield were academicians—Bailey, dean of Cornell's School of Agriculture and Butterfield, a pioneer rural sociologist of the University of Massachusetts. Pennsylvania conservationist Gifford Pinchot, Iowa farm editor and future Secretary of Agriculture Henry C. Wallace, and William A. Beard, editor of California's *Great West Magazine,* represented East, Middle West, and West. Walter Hines Page and Charles S. Barrett of Georgia, who was president of the militant Farmers' Educational and Cooperative Union, the successor to the Farmers' Alliance, were the southerners on the Commission. Barrett, whose appointment was pressed upon a reluctant Roosevelt, got on poorly with his intellectual colleagues and contributed little to the Commission's final report, which Barrett probably considered irrelevant to farming.

Consistent with their scientific concerns, Bailey and Butterfield were also sensitive humanists and philosophers of rural living. Bailey, who introduced modern botany and home economics to farm people, believed in a semireligious relationship between man and nature; he feared the mania for efficiency and systematization which businessmen preached. Walter Hines Page, a former farm boy who had fled to the cities himself, nonetheless shared his contemporaries' devotion to farm life. Page decried the continuing rural exodus, mourned the farm's loss of its young, and used his *World's Work* to stimulate a national "back to the land" movement.

The Commission held its hearings across the country and published its brief report in 1909. Somewhat after the fashion of urban muckrakers, the Commissioners hoped that discussion, fact-gathering, and reports would generate improvements in conditions. They made few demands for legislation, even in respect to the regulation of railroads and agricultural middlemen. Instead, the report stressed self-help. This commendable but ineffectual commentary was typical: "The liquor question has been emphasized to the Commission in all parts of the country as complicating the labor problem. It seems to be regarded as a burning country life problem. Intemperance is largely the result of the barrenness of farm

life, particularly of the lot of the hired man." "The saloon,"
therefore, "must be banished from at least all country districts and rural towns if our agricultural interests are to develop. . . . The evil is specially damning in the South, because
it seriously complicates the race problem." The Commission
called upon "every person to exert his best effort to provide
the open country with such intellectual and social interests
as will lessen the appeal and attractiveness of the saloon."

However, the Commission did produce results—some direct
and forceful, others more innocuous. In Raleigh, Commission
sanitarian Dr. Charles W. Stiles alerted his audience to the
hookworm menace, prescribed the cure, and soon convinced
directors of the Rockefeller Foundation to finance an educa-
tion-eradication program. Commission hearings and subsequent Country Life Association activities also promoted more
farmers' institutes, where agriculture professors lectured
farmers on the latest techniques and equipment. Interest in
the new discipline of rural sociology heightened; the Commission report became a text in the field. Governors proclaimed "Farmers' Weeks" in North Carolina and other
southern states. During such observances, farmers' institutes
discussed the enrichment of country living and scientific
farming. A late 1908 Country Life Conference at the University of Virginia—attended by delegates from throughout the
Southeast—was followed by the founding of state country life
conferences in Wisconsin (1911), West Virginia (1912), Mis-
souri (1913), and elsewhere. Rural sociologists and urban
editors of such magazines as *World's Work, Outlook, Independent,* and *Survey* were the prime initiators. They formed
the heart and supplied the enthusiasm for the American
Country Life Association—and more generally, for what Bailey
called the "country life movement." The Association and the
movement flourished throughout the progressive era, holding
a climactic national conference in 1919.

The movement was nostalgic and full of uplifting sentiments. Nevertheless, its enthusiasts had problems. They set

out originally to save the countryside as a bastion of the values of old America in order that the cities might be saved. Here was a pure and moral goal. Increasingly, however, as country life reformers studied the rural condition of the country, their meetings, speeches, and publications became more oriented toward the scientific and "business" aspects of farming as ends in themselves. Country life and efficient farming techniques had ever complemented one another; there was no natural conflict. Yet, during the progressive years, farming inexorably became more of a way to earn a living and somewhat less of a transcendant way of life.

Seaman Asahel Knapp was the most significant contributor to improved southern agriculture.[4] He was born on a frontier subsistence farm near Lake Champlain, New York in 1833. Knapp struggled for his classical education at Union College, from which he emerged a "professor" of ancient languages and taught in various academies in his native state and in Pennsylvania. Ordained a Methodist minister, he combined an idealistic sense of mission with practicality, hard work, and an indominable physical constitution. However, shortly after the Civil War, an accident left him with a stiff knee and a physician's warning that his sedentary pedagogical pursuits would result in a deterioration of his condition. Knapp abandoned his career, uprooted his young family, and removed to a farm outside Vinton, near Cedar Rapids, Iowa.

The first prairie winter annihilated Knapp's flock of pedigreed sheep, which were to have been the basis of his farming activities. For a time thereafter he was reduced to common "dirt farming"—a semicripple riding the plow, his crutches hanging on one handle. Yet, the hardy Yankee survived, preaching at the local Methodist church and presiding over a nearby school for the blind. During his financial and physical recovery, Knapp educated himself in the latest methods of practical husbandry and agriculture through reading eastern and European farm journals and scientific reports. This experience taught him that an investment in the very best animals, seed, and equipment, and adherence to the latest "book methods" of farm management, brought the greatest returns in the long run.

In the mid-1870s, Knapp purchased ten expensive Poland-China breeder hogs from southwestern Ohio. Disdaining the slop and wallow husbandry of his neighbors, Knapp housed, fed, and bred his pigs with greater care than was given most of his neighbors' children. Greater animal weights, profits, and long-run economies justified his methods. The farmer-businessman and inveterate preacher than began to proselytize. The breeder needed customers; Iowa's husbandry must be improved; peddlers of inferior scrub animals must be excluded from the state. This combination of ideals and self-interest led Knapp in turn to cofound the *Iowa Stock Journal* (which he edited for a time) and also a state breeders' association. He successfully lobbied through these vehicles for state legislation protecting pure-breeders against the frauds of scrub sellers. Knapp also founded a bank at Vinton which reduced farm mortgage rates and financed farmers who wished to improve their stock. James ("Tama Jim") Wilson (later McKinley's and Roosevelt's Secretary of Agriculture), and the first "Uncle Henry" Wallace, whose family later assumed ownership of Knapp's *Stock Journal* (renamed *Wallace's Farmer*) and produced two secretaries of agriculture—were close neighbors and colleagues in this early crusade for progressive agriculture.

Knapp's expanding. activities as an exponent of practical science in farming next led him to Ames, Iowa, as a professor in the growing Iowa Agriculture College. There he worked out his learn-by-doing agricultural pedagogy, a middle western counterpart to General Samuel C. Armstrong's Hampton Institute formula. In addition, he experimented with new seed, administered buildings and grounds, and finally served as president of the institution for a brief time in the mid-1880s. In the meantime Knapp's work and lobbying among local congressmen helped win the enactment of the Hatch Experiment Station Act in 1887.

While president of the college at Ames, Knapp began negotiations for yet another career with land developer-entrepreneur Jabez B. Watkins. Watkins had secured more than a million acres of swampy wastelands and barren prairie in southwestern Louisiana, which he had already begun to drain by use of new steam-powered dredging equipment. The costly, grandiose project would attract settlers and earn grand profits if properly publicized by an imaginative, trusted, scientific agriculturist. Knapp was offered sufficient salary, latitude, and speculative opportunity to be induced to uproot his family once more and move to Lake Charles in 1887. This decision was a critical juncture in the development of southern agriculture.

At Lake Charles, Knapp once more became a banker and founded yet another farm magazine, the *Rice Journal*. The bank helped provide mortgage money for settlers on Watkins-Knapp land, and the *Journal* educated immigrant Yankees and native Cajuns in an informed approach to rice culture, particularly in the revolutionary application of steam and horse-powered wheat harvesting and threshing machinery to rice crops. Knapp also established a rice mill and learned that milling machinery damaged up to 60 percent of rice kernels prior to marketing. Knapp decided that finding more resistant rice was more practical than developing new mills and, with an appropriation from Secretary of Agriculture "Tama Jim" Wilson, he set out on his first tour of the Orient in search of hardier strains of rice. His "Kyushu" seed, after successful experimentation in Louisiana, reduced kernel breakage by more than 50 percent.

At the turn of the century, Knapp's friendship with Wilson led to his appointment—with a tiny subsidy—as the Department's Special Agent for the Promotion of Agriculture in the South. The dreaded Mexican boll weevil had crossed the Rio Grande and was ravaging the cotton fields of neighboring Texas. The best defense seemed to lie in the development of resistant cotton strains and crop diversification. Knapp's experience in Iowa farming and farmer-education led him to establish and supervise federally-owned model farms in order to demonstrate the alternatives of crop rotation and better seed. However, the models were failures; Knapp discovered that provincial dirt farmers were suspicious of Washington-financed and operated programs and believed scientific procedures untrustworthy and beyond their reach.

On a farm near Terrell, Texas in 1902, Knapp finally discovered the formula for the successful propagation of scientific agriculture. There the local business community offered an "insurance fund" against failure to a local farmer, provided that Knapp would supply the latest information and serve as "scientific" counsellor. Knapp accepted; the local farmer planted tested seed, rotated crops, diversified, fertilized, and netted $700 above his usual return. On the basis of this experiment Knapp was deluged with requests for advice for owner-operated demonstration farms throughout the South.

During 1903-1904 Knapp worked out the Farmers' Cooperative Demonstration Work Program, which was headquartered in Washington in the Department of Agriculture's Bureau of Plant Industry and financed by the federal government, the states, and the Rockefeller-endowed General Education Board. Funds from Knapp's office went mainly to hire demonstration agents on the county level, the "Gabriels" of the new farm methodology. The county agents' tasks were both simple and monumental: to persuade backward southern farmers to abandon single-staple agriculture, diversify and rotate crops, and use ample fertilizer and good, tested seed—in other words, to break out of the vicious economic spiral of staple overproduction, low prices, excessive debt, land ruination, and human deprivation. Successful agents had to be masters of country diplomacy and careful to respect farmers' rustic dignity; furthermore, they must never "talk down," and must prove every case by demonstration and hard evidence. This horseback teaching, backed by fear-easing "failure insurance" funds which were raised in many ways in various parts of the region, began the slow redemption of southern agriculture.

What Knapp did was to begin to close a great gulf that had always separated the common farmer from the traditional and modern practical knowledge that had somehow never filtered down to him. Thomas Jefferson and his son-in-law had known about and practiced crop rotation and contour plowing on Monticello, but most postbellum cotton farmers slaved in ignorance. Knapp's genius was knowledge transmission. He created the modern county agent system which, along with other factors, contributed over many years finally to reverse the misery of the southern farmer.

When, in 1911, Knapp died in harness at the age of seventy-seven, congressmen and senators were already deep in debate over legislation to nationalize and institutionalize the county agent system. The Smith-Lever Act, finally passed in 1914, climaxed the work of the grim, energetic adopted southerner. The progressive era, now in its Wilsonian phase, thus brought to fruition not only urban reform but the long-frustrated demands for agricultural improvement.

Individuals across the South followed Seaman Knapp and fostered a new agriculture for a wide variety of reasons. Some became "scientific" agriculturists because of essentially old-fashioned, "Jeffersonian" goals. Like Clarence Poe, Liberty Hyde Bailey, and Theodore Roosevelt in his more florid moments, they began with the premise that farming was a superior lifestyle and, secondarily perhaps, a means of making a living. Application of scientific techniques and implementation of governmental regulations were to them a means of saving the rural way of life. Others still cherished country living but came closer to seeing agriculture as simply a kind of business enterprise. James Willard Ragsdale, Asbury Francis ("A. Frank") Lever, and Claude Kitchin —congressional colleagues from the Carolinas—well represented this group.

After working for a railroad, Ragsdale attended the University of South Carolina, prepared for law, and became a

sort of potentate in the neighborhood of Florence, South
Carolina. In addition to his career as an impetuous jury
lawyer, he was a planter, a banker, and a small-time
financier. Politically, he was a staunch Tillman man. His
oratory, according to James F. Byrnes, carried the state
Democratic convention for Woodrow Wilson in 1912; in
Congress he supported New Freedom legislation that seemed
to attack big business and restore competition by creating
safety and opportunity for small business, provincial banking,
and farming. Ragsdale's small-town and country world was
under attack; he had interests to protect and, because of his
interests, he could readily see the interdependency of farming
and business.[3]

A. Frank Lever worked on an upcountry farm as a boy,
struggled through Newberry College, and taught school for
a time. In 1899, he finished law school at Georgetown University in Washington, while holding a position as private
secretary to a congressman. After serving a term in the state
house of representatives, he defeated four Democratic primary opponents and went to Congress himself. He was then
only twenty-six years old. Finally, in the footsteps of Tillman, Lever promoted state and federal aid to rural people
and assailed the trusts. He became identified with the movement to extend Knapp's demonstration work as a member
of the House's agriculture committee and chairman of the
committee on education. In 1911, he introduced one of the
early bills proposing a federal county agent system, and
the final 1914 Smith-Lever Act immortalized him in the
annals of American agriculture.

Claude Kitchin, the "radical" from Scotland Neck, North
Carolina, also fit the small-town, small business mold. Kitchin was a farmer, lawyer, and president of his town's
Planter's and Commercial Bank which, in 1914 claimed only
$150 thousand in resources. He also combined an enmity
toward bigness and "monopoly" with a versatile, practical
bent which comprehended efficient agriculture. Better farming meant better business for the provincial middle class.

Virginia's William Hodges Mann was a solid rural progressive on the state level. Born in 1843 to a middle class Williamsburg family, he served as an enlisted man in the Confederate army, then studied law and moved west to Nottoway County, near Petersburg, Virginia. He was elected county judge in 1870, while still a very young man. He occupied the local bench for the rest of the century and also engaged in farming, legal consultations, banking, and real estate (timber and coal) speculation. Mann went to the state senate in 1899 and immediately identified with agricultural issues, education, and the surging prohibition movement. He helped found the Virginia Anti-Saloon League in 1901 with his friend James Cannon; in addition, a local option law which bore his name paved the way toward a dry rural Virginia.

As the candidate of Senator Thomas Martin's state machine, Mann was elected governor in 1909. The county agent system grew and flourished, along with experiment station work at the Virginia Polytechnic Institute, during his administration. Mann was largely responsible for creating the state United Agricultural Board which coordinated agent and extension work financed privately and by the state and federal governments; the Board smoothed over the transition to the future Smith-Lever system. Mann also gave his support to a popular and somewhat radical (for Virginia) measure to have the state crush limestone and sell it cheaply to farmers as fertilizer. An elderly Victorian and an inflexible moralist with a patriarchal white beard, Mann knew that the latest technology and even new political ideas were essential to preserve and improve the old Virginia that was familiar and dear to him.

Alabama's old Populist warrior, Reuben F. Kolb, also innovated. Kolb was a typical all-cotton farmer until he went broke in the 1880s. He found salvation in his watermelon patch, where his "Kolb's Gem" earned such popularity that he did a flourishing seed business during the worst of the hard times. "Kolb's Gem" was the result of considerable experimentation which sold Kolb and his admirers on scientific agriculture. In the late 1880s and again in the progressive era (after he made peace with the Democrats), Kolb served as state commissioner of agriculture; he used his position to promote farmers' institutes, the dissemination of experiment information, and the county agent system.

Georgia's Hoke Smith was a North Carolina-born son of an impoverished professor who knew little of farm life. At an early age his family moved to Atlanta, that materialist mecca of the New South which was his home thereafter. Urbanite Smith practiced law and politics—with and against corporations. He was four-square opposed to Tom Watson's Populists and their agrarian Democratic fellow travelers and became a staunch Grover Cleveland supporter—a conservative "gold bug" on the vital currency question of the 1890s. Cleveland rewarded his efforts with the secretaryship of the interior. However, once Smith had helped lay to rest rural radicalism, his ambition and his public spirit combined to make him a progressive reformer. In order to win statewide elections, he had to become a trust-buster and support corporate regulation, public schools, racial extremism, and other essentially country policies—although prohibition was most difficult for him to swallow. Therefore, in 1905-1906 he combined with his old enemy Watson, roused the crackers on the race issue and, as governor, presided over the culmination of Georgia's disfranchisement movement. The white-collared Atlantan learned to commune with the rural white masses; in this practical fashion, Smith—as a United States Senator—sponsored A. Frank Lever's bill in the upper house and also became immortal in the annals of progressive agriculture.

B. B. Comer was a stern southern Yankee, made of the stuff which generates industrial revolution and sweat shops. He was born in rural Alabama in 1848; after college in Virginia he returned to the Lower South and launched a successful career in cotton planting and manufacturing. He was major owner of the Avondale and Central mills of

Birmingham and of extensive farm acreage. Ruthless and energetic, he exploited child labor in mills which were characterized by Alexander McKelway as among the worst he had seen. Yet Comer became a reformer. As a planter and manufacturer, he felt victimized by railroads which freighted his crops and products, and these grievances drove him into politics. He served as president of the state railroad commission in 1905-1906 and became interested in prohibition, another mainly rural-oriented issue which he embraced with vigor, lumping together the distillers and the railroad companies as "interests" who must not be allowed "to run the state." Now a full-fledged progressive, he was elected governor and served from 1907 to 1910.

While Comer was significant as another rural-style moralist, he was also typical of the Lower South farmers upon whom the Knapp approach to agriculture made almost an immediate impact. Literate, well traveled, and business-minded, they readily adapted themselves to new information and techniques, and possessed the capital to put it all together. However, the masses of Lower South farmers were ignorant and uninterested because they were tenants; they were virtually untouched by Knapp's work and the deluge of farm information which was effective only where agriculture was healthier. Thus, Comer and like-minded planters were the exception. Even before the Mexican boll weevil reached Alabama, Comer had developed a model of modern, efficient operations, prudently reducing his cotton acreage and diversifying with fruit trees, pecans, peanuts, and purebred livestock. One looks in vain for rhapsodies to rural living in his papers and speeches. He seems, rather, to have regarded diversification simply as common sense and shrewd business.

John M. Parker represented the extreme example of the businessman-as-agriculturist. Born in Mississippi in 1863, he went into the New Orleans cotton brokerage business as a young man. At the age of forty, he was a substantial banker-warehouseman-shipper, a railroad executive, and an owner of extensive alluvial acreage in Mississippi and Louisiana. He was a New Orleans grandee, active in social and business associations, and a believer in clean government. Parker also advocated the protective tariff and "absolute control by the Federal Government, of the Mississippi River and its tributaries, to prevent overflow and disaster." Factorage and factory-style cotton agriculture were inseparably bound; they were essential to the region. The river was paramount, but local government and private citizens could not maintain the complex of levees; thus, the necessity of rational control, planning, and maintenance by the national government. Alexander Hamilton, Henry Clay, and scores of Delta planter-businessmen before him had reasoned similarly.

Originally a Democrat, Parker was drawn to Theodore Roosevelt's personality and to his economic nationalism. In 1912, he was a principal organizer of the Louisiana Progressive Party and sought to attract—as always—"the very best class of citizens." Before the party collapsed just prior to the general election of 1916, Roosevelt and national Progressives picked Parker—preeminent among the elite group of southern Progressives—as their vice-presidential candidate. Switching back to the Democrats, Parker hastily endorsed Wilson and ran for governor. Parker suffered lampooning as a racial equalitarian at the hands of the Democrats, because he was tainted by his flirtations with erstwhile "black" Republicans of the North. Democratic enemies also exploited D. W. Griffith's new film, "Birth of a Nation," insinuating that Parker and evil old Thad Stevens of Reconstruction days were of the same ilk. That Louisiana Progressives were officially opposed to "anarchy" and committed to maintenance of "white man's rule" was of little consequence. In 1920, Parker returned to the gubernatorial fray, won, and attempted to guide the state by his gentleman-businessman's code of honor. So trusting was he of his own class that he invited Standard Oil lawyers to write severance tax legislation. This bit of "best people" solidarity would provoke a protracted hassle with a young upcountry politician named Huey P. Long.

However, Parker's nationalist vision, his power, and his innovative acumen in business affairs, were the stuff of which new agricultural departures were made in the bleak Lower South. Like Comer, the patrician Louisianian saw doom in cotton and, given the additional goad of the advancing boll weevil, Parker early began to diversify, particularly to beef cattle production. This departure from single staple agriculture by men such as Parker was particularly significant because of their wide influence and position. Parker put the theme of diversification into speeches he made on the political stump and on the rostrums of the Southern Commercial Congress (which he served as president), the New Orleans Board of Trade, and other associations.

Contrary to their storied image of disdain for hayseeds and their distance from farming, businessmen—bankers, brokers, jobbers, railroad executives—took a sustaining interest in Knapp's work and played a critical role in the transition to scientific agriculture. Knapp's own banking, publishing, and real estate interests have already been noted. Enlightened self-interest also prompted hundreds of other bankers, investors, railroad directors, and chambers of commerce to promote modern, businesslike farming throughout the South and the nation. The corporate-funded Rosenwald and Rockefeller foundations helped subsidize southern county agents in the critical early years, and individual local businessmen—large and small—contributed heavily of their time and money, from Terrell, Texas to Caroline County, Virginia. Better farming meant more business for everyone. Railroads in the South and Middle West provided institute trains which brought farm exhibits and university experts to rural areas. W. W. Finley, Southern Railway president, enthusiastically financed and organized "farmers' specials" all along his lines. Better crop yields meant more freight and more conspicuous consumption along those lines. The American

Bankers' Association, the National Implement and Vehicle Association, the National Association of Retailers, the American Steel and Wire Company, and most railway corporations were conspicuous supporters of the Smith-Lever bill. Bringing expertise into agriculture became nearly everyone's passion. Not the least among many benefits would be a prosperous, contented people, safe and conservative.[4]

In the Lower South the educated, more prosperous farmers and planters readily realized the blessings of science and diversification. Comer, Parker and other "planter statesmen" enthusiastically tried to lead an agricultural "revolution," but one without socioeconomic dislocation, redistribution of land, or serious discomfort to themselves. Their ambition was greater profits within the economic status quo. Knapp's demonstration work and his scientific agriculture did not, could not, cure many of the essential ills of the cotton South: the credit shortage, the crop lien system, the persistence of poverty, disease, and ignorance. There would be no revolution, perhaps partially because of the false hopes held out by the new agriculture. Instead, a depression, a Tennessee Valley Authority, World War II, massive suffering and migrations to cities and the North, and accelerated southern industrialization would all painfully transpire before the gradual recovery of farming in the late 1950s and 1960s.

Areas not in the clutches of a staple culture, mainly in the Upper South, responded more readily to the new farm methods. Virginia was an excellent case in point. Already a diversified state (except for the tobacco staple of the south-central section), the Old Dominion did not suffer the extreme conditions prevailing in the cotton belt. Available statistics indicate a decided upswing in farm fortunes during the progressive era. Between 1900 and 1913, Virginia farm land doubled in value; the total farm value (land, buildings, equipment, and products) increased 132 percent—an impressive rate despite inflation. More interesting (and unsouthern) was a steady diminishing of the size of the average owned farm between 1870 and 1911: from 245 to 106 acres. Considering that Virginia was the only southern state to achieve an actual decline in tenancy, it would seem that the family-sized and family-owned farm was reappearing.[5]

These relatively good times produced soaring aspirations and a new professionalism among farmers. However, this increased ambition also made them discontented with the pace of their material progress. Editorials and letters published in the state's principal farm journal, the *Southern Planter* (Richmond), repeated one persistent theme; editor J. F. Jackson, a polished English immigrant to the Old Dominion, bemoaned in unison with his zealous correspondents the "sad state" of the countryside. "Nearly everywhere is manifest," wrote one observer, "a lack of the useful information contained in your valuable publication." Another letter writer complained of "the old methods here in vogue," prescribing, like everyone, science and businesslike farm management as cures. They reasoned that science had made the manufacturers successful and "progressive" through the application of science to their "business." In 1908, a positive-thinking northern Virginia planter-dairyman proudly announced: "The listless, I may say hopeless, farmer of yesterday has seen a new light and has become the bustling man of affairs of to-day. No longer is he content with the old conditions and methods, for he is steadily mustering and applying along agricultural lines what scientific research has brought to his aid."

One source of the science fetish in Virginia was the state Department of Agriculture and Immigration. The department was generally ineffective before 1904, when it entered into cooperation with the Virginia Polytechnic Institute's agriculture faculty and the testing station at Blacksburg. This long-delayed combination soon produced a thorough soil study of the commonwealth and, more important, the publication of bulletins presenting the latest information from the testing station and the Department. If statistics are a fair indicator of farmers' voracious appetite for technical data, there is little doubt that a new era had arrived: public demand drove

circulation of the bulletins from 200 thousand in 1906 to
nearly a million in 1912.

In addition to providing agricultural bulletins the Department began in 1900 to provide partial subsidies for a new
phenomenon in the Virginia countryside—institute trains. The
Southern and the Norfolk & Western railways dispatched
"moving laboratories" through rural areas during the winter;
these were stocked with farm exhibits and staffed by lec-
turers from the Polytechnic Institute. Institute train ar-
rivals at isolated rail sidings were always important local
events. Bands played; ladies packed box lunches, and chau-
tauqua style speeches flourished. The "new agriculture" came
to country folk in this manner until the trains were discon-
tinued in 1914, following passage of the Smith-Lever Act.

Knapp's Demonstration Work and Boys' Corn Clubs, a sort
of junior auxiliary, came to the Old Dominion in 1907; both
were under the direction of T. O. Sandy, a native of Burke-
ville. Three years later, the federal program was combined
administratively with the state agriculture department and,
in 1914, Governor Mann created the United Agricultural
Board as liaison between the vast assistance and information
resources of the federal government and the thousands of
science enthusiasts on the farms. By 1916, 64 agents served
Virginia's 100 counties. A smoothly operating administration
—a marvel of federal-state cooperation that would have been
incomprehensible a few years before—became a reality.

T. O. Sandy was typical of progressive farm leaders in
the first decade of the new century. Born during the 1860s,
Sandy was a diligent man who, through study and experimentation, converted his own wornout farm into a lush
agricultural showplace. He became an ardent testimonialist
to the blessings of crop rotation and fertilizer, and his
leadership of the Demonstration Work in Virginia gave him
an opportunity to spread the gospel of legumes, stock
breeding, and continued diversification. Sandy also served
in 1907 and 1908 as president of the Virginia State Farmers'
Institute, a private group of about 200 active members

which was originally formed in 1904. The Farmers' Institute was a studious and gentlemanly society, in the best tradition of Old Dominion scientific farmer organizations; under Sandy's inspired hand, it added force to the education movement.

Sandy's general outlook was even more significant than his emphasis upon practical education. Like John Taylor and Jefferson before him, he was a dead-serious spokesman of country life, who sincerely feared the "moral depravity" of cities and hoped that he might somehow reverse the trend toward urbanization by revitalizing the farm. That improved technology had given impetus to both urbanization and modern farming tools and techniques apparently did not occur to him. Like his contemporary Clarence Poe, Sandy sought old-fashioned ends with new-fangled means.

Westmoreland Davis, who succeeded Sandy as president of the Farmers' Institute in 1909, was of quite different background and philosophy. Born in 1859, Davis left his boyhood home of Richmond in the mid-1880s for New York City, where he became a successful corporation lawyer. After fifteen years of exposure to that highly systematized environment, Davis retired from the law and returned to Virginia in 1903. He purchased an old plantation on the Potomac near Washington, D. C., and became a "farmer" for the first time at the age of forty-four. Davis, who was an unusually energetic and versatile man, rapidly absorbed the current enthusiasm for progressive farming, used his considerable resources to build a model, highly productive, dairy and stock farm, and emerged as an organizational leader among farmers. His rise to leadership of the Farmers' Institute was preceded by his cofounding of the Virginia Dairymen's Association in late 1907.

Davis was an advocate of practical education, but he was even more interested in galvanizing farmers into a powerful interest group which could make its influence felt within the ruling Democratic party and the legislature. In an age of speed, bigness, and vast, contending power structures, Davis

believed that businesslike organization was the key to effective representation and protection. Manufacturers, laborers,
and the professions had organized; the time for "businessmen" who happened to be farmers was past due. Davis, more
than anyone else, fostered the concepts and practice of
business agriculture in Virginia and the Upper South.

He was not inspired by the Populist heritage, the new
Farmers' Union, or the country life movement; rather, he was
excited by the sophisticated business whirl of New York
and the advanced agricultural states of the Middle West,
particularly Wisconsin. In 1911, during a visit to Madison,
Davis became acquainted firsthand with the Wisconsin Idea
while auditing lectures by economist John R. Commons and
touring the university's College of Agriculture. Briefly the
"Idea" stated that "the boundary of the University is the
boundary of the state." Under President Charles Van Hise
and Governor Robert La Follette, the University of Wisconsin advanced the theory that modern society's complex
problems required the skill of experts. The state, therefore,
would generously support its institution of higher learning
and, in return, the expertise of the university would be made
available to the state at large. In Wisconsin, this formula had
helped catalyze the remarkable transition of that state's
economy from unprofitable wheat growing on wornout land
to the rich dairy industry for which Wisconsin became
famous.

Even though the institute trains and agricultural bulletins
had made some inroads, state aid to a farming interest
group conflicted ideologically with the Old Dominion's
cherished tradition—however fraudulent—of laissez-faire. Davis
countered the state rights and "rugged individualism" legacy
of an older era by rudely setting out to shock the state with
his concept of neomercantilism. He told the 1909 Farmers'
Institute meeting: "We must abandon in our school of
economics the austere individualism that has created an
aristocracy of wealth, and set in motion the benign methods
of aided individualism, which offer opportunity . . . not in

agriculture alone, but in all the walks of life. England, Ireland, France, Germany, and the Progressive Northwestern states have blazed the way; we have but to profit by their experience and example."

Davis took charge of the Farmers' Institute and, within a year, transformed it from a genteel education society into an effective lobbying organization. In 1910, the incoming assembly was greeted by the Institute's articulate legislative committee headed by Davis; by the close of 1916, an impressive array of progressive bills had been passed: a seed inspection law; the establishment of the Torrens system of land registration; an authorization for cooperatives to aid the work of the new Virginia branch of the Farmers' Union. The legislature also provided additional funds for construction of rural roads and schools and for bounties on animals which destroyed crops; it also required the bonding of commission merchants handling agricultural products. An innocuous-appearing "ice cream act" in 1912 actually fulfilled a major goal of the Virginia Dairymen's Association and the Farmers' Institute. The law required ice cream which was made with any dairy product other than fresh cow's milk to be clearly labeled as such. The intent of the legislation was to discriminate against dried or condensed dairy products imported from other states (notably Wisconsin); dairymen thus hoped to foster a home state dairy industry comparable to Wisconsin's. In 1914 the Farmers' Institute secured creation of a legislative reference bureau. Davis himself wrote the bureau bill, basing it upon Wisconsin and New Jersey models. The reference bureau would exist independently within the state library, providing information and legal expertise to "farmer legislators" who lacked legal training.

In 1912 Davis purchased the *Southern Planter* and made the journal a fierce partisan of specific legislation and an enemy of politicians not attuned to the "new agriculture." ' Davis was instrumental in the formation of the Agricultural Conference, a farm-problem caucus, in the General Assembly in 1914. The Agricultural Conference was only loosely organized and operated more under the inspiration of Davis, the *Southern Planter*, the Farmers' Institute, and the allied Farmers' Union than under the tutelage. of the state Democratic political organization. Opposition to the Conference usually came from the representatives of economic interest groups which were sometimes adversely affected by farm legislation. This, as we shall see below, was especially true in the Senate, the bastion of railroad and manufacturing interests.

The crowning achievement of farmer progressivism in Virginia was its victory in the protracted controversy over lime. If Old Dominion farm land had needed calcium in Edmund Ruffin's day—the first half of the nineteenth century—the need was even more critical in the early twentieth century. Interestingly, as the momentum of the farmers' movement intensified, attention once more centered upon Ruffin's chemistry. The most readily accessible source of usable calcium was limestone, found in deposits virtually everywhere in the western part of the state. Manufacturers quarried, then "burnt" the stone in kilns for shipment to farmers as fertilizer. Burnt lime, consisting of up to 98 percent calcium oxide, quickly turned to calcium carbonate when applied to freshly plowed ground. In hastening the decay of vegetation, lime "sweetened" the acid condition so common to Virginia's soils. After this treatment, even the most wornout land in the tidewater could grow humus-producing legumes and, in rotation, rich crops of corn, hay, or nearly any suitable staple.

What made lime a frustrating problem was its price · At a Virginia kiln burnt lime sold for about $4.85 per ton; high railway rates added to farmers' costs. Because each acre needed three-quarters to one ton of lime, most farmers found the cure too expensive. However, by 1909, an apparent solution to the dilemma had been demonstrated in Illinois, one of Davis's "Progressive Northwestern States." A few years before, Illinois' legislature had authorized the establishment of a state-owned, convict-worked limestone grinding plant.

At very low cost, it produced ground limestone (100 pounds of which is equal in effect to 56ᴵ pounds of burnt lime) and sold it at the plant for 60¢ per ton. Illinois railroads, in turn, had been persuaded to ship the lime to farmers at one-half cent per ton per mile.

With farm leaders already convinced of the great need for lime in Virginia, Westmoreland Davis traveled to Illinois in late 1909, studied the lime industry of the state firsthand; consequently, in January of the following year, the Farmers' Institute petitioned the Virginia assembly for a reproduction of the Illinois limestone grinding plant and freight rate.

Despite opposition from the Richmond lobby of the National Lime Manufacturers' Association of Virginia, the limestone grinding bill easily passed the lower house. The bill faltered, however, in the Senate. During the two-year interregnum before the 1912 legislative session, there was a battle of interest groups—"limeburners" on the one hand and the Farmers' Institute and Farmers' Union on the other. Davis excoriated the "limeburners" in typically progressive rhetoric as a nefarious "trust" and an "arrogant and insolent body of alien and mercenary manufacturers." The lime manufacturers maintained that the farmers' bill was "socialistic" and unconstitutional because it would place the state in competition with private enterprise. Nevertheless, with the support of "Farmer Governor" William H. Mann, the assembly authorized two plants in 1912. The farmer-lobbyists had won.

Nevertheless, the "limeburners" and railroads refused to give up. The lime manufacturers petitioned the Virginia Supreme Court of Appeals and, not until January 1914, was the act declared constitutional. In the meantime Governor Mann, Davis, and other agricultural leaders met with railway presidents, hoping to achieve voluntary. compliance with the "Illinois rate" of one-half cent per ton per mile on ground limestone. The farmers were obliged to seek a coercive order from the State Corporation Commission because only two of the nine roads operating in the state voluntarily complied. This action consumed a year; a favorable decision came finally in May of 1915 and the first lime plant began operations in mid-1915. Despite these delays, the ultimate prevalence of the "Illinois rate" and the opening of the first plant seemed like victory at Armageddon to the rural people. "Lime, Legumes, And Then Anything You Want To Grow" was the *Southern Planter's* fulfilled "watchword of progress and the new civilization to be."

With a successful legislative session in 1916, Davis's election as governor in 1917, and American entry into the world war, the farmers' progressive movement, having achieved most of its major goals—was submerged by larger events. In a decade and a half, country people had embraced the promises of science and technology. Eschewing third-party politics, they adopted the more effective lobby—the modern interest group form of politicoeconomic agitation. Given this tool and the advantages of fine leadership and better conditions than in the cotton belt, Virginia farmers were more successful than other reformers. For them, education and self-help—the American Way—really worked.

VIII

PROGRESSIVISM IN BLACK

*The only real "open door" . . . for [Negroes] . . .
evidently is the farm.*

R. R. WRIGHT, 1900

IN a way, black people did not participate in southern
progressivism. This was because white progressivism originated in a racial settlement. Yet, if the turn-of-the-century
marked a distinctive era for whites, it was certainly also a
definable epoch for blacks: it was the nadir of their postemancipation existence in America. With one of their number
lynched or burned somewhere every other day and, with the
federal government, the Republican party, and the northern
white public acquiescing in the white South's aggressions
against them, Negroes withdrew into themselves and prepared to weather the long ordeal. Yet, even in withdrawal,
they launched their own "progressive" reforms.[1]

William Edward Burghardt DuBois, for example, during his
early Atlanta University career (1897-1909) was in many
respects a classic progressive type. Born in western Massachusetts in 1868, he was educated in history and sociology
at Fisk, Harvard, and in Germany. Aristocratic of mien,
DuBois was a successful product of graduate school discipline; he believed in "scientific" fact-gathering and publication as an efficacious means of demonstrating social evil

and bringing about redress. He had the same faith during these years as contemporary white muckrakers, who systematically exposed urban slum conditions, governmental corruption, and bad working conditions.

Up until 1905, when he joined civil rights militants in the Niagara Movement, DuBois restricted himself primarily to scholarly fact-gathering, as other muckraking progressives did. Perhaps the limited returns of such detached but worthy labor helped drive DuBois into political activism and radicalism: he became a socialist before he left Atlanta for New York in 1909. In the meantime, however, he and his student associates produced a number of immensely valuable volumes in the Atlanta University Publications series, including *The Negro Family in the United States, The Negro Businessman*, and *The Negro Artisan* (all DuBois-edited). He closely studied rural cotton belt blacks, publishing some of his findings and impressions in his famed *Souls of Black Folk*. In the same period, he produced his classic urban study, *The Philadelphia Negro*. Virtually all this work, in its wealth of detail, implicitly called for reform without revolution.

An emigré to New York, William Lewis Bulkley, was probably the most important southern black progressive. Born a slave in South Carolina at the beginning of the Civil War, he worked his way through Claflin University, then went north for graduate work at Wesleyan University and at Syracuse, where he earned a doctorate in classics in 1893. He returned to his home state and taught for a while at Claflin until, angry and intimidated by Tillman's white supremacy campaign and the new state constitution, he left for New York City. He taught there in the public schools for several years and in 1899, he became the principal of P. S. 80, a predominantly white school in a transitional neighborhood. Here Bulkley saw the early northward stream of fellow southern blacks who, unlike himself, possessed no urban-related skills or experience. Too often they were also illiterate. Consequently, Bulkley established a day-care center for the children of working mothers and a night school for adult illiterates which also offered courses in job-related subjects.

Bulkley moved into the headstreams of Negro urban reform. In 1906 he founded the Commission for Improving the Industrial Condition of the Negro in New York. The CIICN was a racially integrated organization (Mary White Ovington and other white social workers were involved), designed to provide a practical way-station for rural blacks from the South; it was an ancestor of the National Urban League (established in 1911). Bulkley, Ovington, and fellow workers promoted special manual training schools and equal employment opportunity for immigrant blacks. Later, in 1909, Bulkley helped found the National Association for the Advancement of Colored People, and he continued his urban resettlement work through the 1920s when, alienated and despairing of success, he moved with his family to Europe, where he died in 1931, an emigré twice over.

The black middle class within the greater South accommodated itself to the emerging rigidity of urban segregation. Self-help—the philosophy commonly associated with Booker T. Washington—evolved quite independently of Washington in the bad decades following Reconstruction's collapse. Having no choice, abandoned blacks sought safety in racial solidarity. The middle class came upon self-help and segregation coincidentally—finding profit in ghetto markets where black consumers had earlier dealt with the white merchants. However, the emerging black middle class rose quickly to its new responsibilities. Beginning in the 1870s, community organizations, lodges, and benevolent societies sprouted throughout the region. Washington's National Negro Business League was itself a symbol of the new class's ethic of cautious responsibility. They were essentially different from white businessmen who favored material progress, clean government, and a strong sense of community—that backbone of progressivism—only in their racial views.

Only once did numbers of the southern urban blacks revolt against the race settlement. Between 1900 and 1906, in more than twenty-five cities, from Richmond and Norfolk to Jackson and San Antonio, they led massive boycotts against streetcar companies, anticipating by half a century Martin Luther King, Jr.'s famed Montgomery bus boycott. The humiliation of segregation was the issue. Beginning about 1900, state and local white governments had passed a rash of ordinances to segregate blacks and whites. Resentful blacks who participated in the ensuing boycotts were led by community organizers who ranged from militant editors such as Richmond's John Mitchell, Jr., to conservative Business Leaguer J. C. Napier of Nashville. Virginia and Tennessee blacks chartered their own separate transportation companies as part of the resistance; however, these and other efforts ultimately failed, partially because of white resistance.[2]

Significantly, the historians of the Negro boycotts term them a "conservative protest." While a remarkable-enough phenomenon which took much courage and persistence on the part of its participants, the boycotts primarily sought to preserve a familiar pattern of life. More importantly, they were demonstrably cautious and nonviolent in tone and tactic. Even militant Mitchell exhorted followers to "be conservative and law-abiding, but to walk." The architects of the boycotts understood well the wisdom of the boycott as a means of protest: it requires safe withdrawal from—rather than confrontation with—the opponents. There were few, if any, suicidal Nat Turners in the movement.

Before 1915, only a small minority of blacks lived in cities. The masses were still in the country, and some remarkable things happened there. From emancipation to the great northward wartime migration, the American Negro population grew from 4.5 to 10 millions; yet, in this period, the percentage of the total remaining in the old slave states declined only 3.3 percent—from 86.6 to 86.3. The southern urban black population grew steadily; yet by 1910, only one in five southern blacks lived in the city. Thus, the typical black American on the eve of World War I was still a southern countryman—probably illiterate, impoverished, and isolated from society in a one- or two-room rural cabin he did not own. He and southern farming were virtually one, and any substantive changes for the good or bad in the agricultural South had to effect him.[3]

The postemancipation plight of the freedmen and the travail of southern agriculture are well-known stories. During Reconstruction, blacks' dreams of "forty acres and a mule" were dashed and—in the long postwar farm-credit drought they, like so many whites—fell victim to the syndrome of rack-rent, crop lien, and sharecropping. By the beginning of the twentieth century thousands remained in virtual peonage under cotton state lien laws. Older agricultural units divided and subdivided as tenancy grew to alarming proportions. In the thirty years after 1880, tenants increased to 50 percent or more of all farmers in South Carolina, Georgia, Alabama, Mississippi, Arkansas, Louisiana, and Texas. North Carolina's and Tennessee's rates rose to above 40 percent by 1910, while only Virginia and Florida experienced small declines. Sympathetic observers despaired for blacks because it was apparent that they, having begun freedom landless and in a hostile environment, must have borne the brunt of the spiraling poverty of the rural South.

For the first time in the history of the census, the Bureau of the Census instructed its enumerators in 1900 to compile complete demographic data by race. They repeated these new procedures in 1910; thus, in the several years following 1910, Americans were for the first time able to gauge accurately the relative position of blacks over a decade. The 1900-1910 statistics buttressed previous reports of increasing peonage among both races in the South. However, new figures on land occupancy and ownership revealed remarkable advances by blacks which alarmed or delighted analysts, depending upon their point of view. Clarence Poe, for instance, responded specifically to these new statistics through his rural segregation campaign in 1913.[4]

Booker T. Washington, who felt that he had had a role in

black rural progress, was gratified by the census figures. In 1911, he reported that the total number of black farmers increased 20 percent (to 887,691)—while the number of white farm operators had grown only 17 percent (to 2,191, 805)—in fifteen southern states between 1900 and 1910. The white farmer growth percentile did not equal that race's overall population growth; therefore, Washington correctly concluded that whites were moving to city and factory, while blacks were apparently taking some of their places at the plow. In some Upper South and border states, such as Virginia, there had been small declines in the numbers of black farmers, but these losses were explanable by relative decreases in the states' overall populations. In the Lower South, Louisiana had lost a great many black farm operators, and Washington was justified in believing that Texas, Arkansas, and Oklahoma were the principal destinations of these emigrés. Georgia experienced the most remarkable increases in black farmers: in 1900, the state's farmers were 63 percent white, 37 percent black; in 1910 the statistics were 58 percent and 42 percent, respectively. In this period, blacks had declined numerically in relation to North Carolina's white population—from 33.3 percent to 31.6 percent; yet, black farmers had grown from 24 to 26 percent of the Tar Heel State's total number of farmers. In South Carolina also, the white population had increased somewhat more than the black; however, black farmers maintained their 55 percent portion of the total number of farmers in the state. Finally, the southern acreage cultivated by blacks increased by four million, while the acreage by whites actually fell off by eleven and a half million. Segregationist Poe had not exaggerated; if the trend persisted, rural southern whites would soon find themselves overwhelmed by the advancing blacks.

If Washington had available to him in late 1911 the complete 1910 statistics, including those on ownership and tenancy, his gratification might have been even less restrained. For despite falling cotton prices, the rising farm failure rate, and the greater white population growth, blacks'

"gains" in agricultural land were not entirely as tenants.
They had maintained their previous gains as tenants and had
outstripped white farmers in the percentage of increased
ownership. This seemed nothing short of remarkable in the
prevailing system. The following two tables illustrate both
increasing tenancy rates (especially among blacks) as well as
the *relative* rise of landowning among blacks compared with
white farmers.

PERCENTAGE DISTRIBUTION OF FARMS
BY COLOR AND TENURE, 1900-1910

	WHITE			COLORED		
		Tenants			Tenants	
	Owners	Cash	Share	Owners	Cash	Share
1900	63.8	10.1	26.1	25.4	36.6	38.0
1910	60.5	10.3	29.2	24.5	32.1	43.4

PERCENTAGE INCREASES BY COLOR
AND TENURE, 1900-1910

		Tenants	
	Owners	Cash	Share
Farms operated by whites	11.4	21.6	29.9
Farms operated by blacks	16.3	5.2	37.0

In other words, during the first decade of the century,
farmers of both races were gravely affected by the continued subdivision of land and rising nonowner cultiva-
tion. White owners declined 3.3 percent (from 63.8 percent
to 60.5 percent) of the total number of white farmers, while
the black landowner percentile fell only 0.9. Given southern
socio-economic conditions, it is not surprising that the black

share of tenancy increases greatly exceeded the white, 37.0 percent to 29.9 percent. However, the phenomenon of the black ownership percentage growth also exceeding white is noteworthy and deserving of investigation.

W. E. B. DuBois, who remains the closest student of black landholding, estimated that the process of acquisition was steady in the post-Civil War decades: "they held about three million acres in 1875, perhaps 8,000,000 in 1890, and 12,000,000 in 1900." Some free blacks had owned property in antebellum times, particularly in the coastal plains of Maryland, Virginia, and North Carolina. Following the war, the Freedmen's Bureau was successful in redistributing some abandoned lands among blacks, although President Andrew Johnson's generosity to former rebels negated landholding hopes for most freedmen. A few of the freedmen took advantage of the Southern Homestead Act to acquire farms on marginal land. However, blacks purchased most of the land they owned in 1875. Outside the black belt, marginal and depleted soil was cheap, and thousands of ambitious black men bought small, poor farms. Still, the acquisition of rich land in the Lower South cotton country was most difficult. Real estate prices remained relatively high, and whites made concerted efforts to block purchases by blacks. DuBois believed that cotton belt Negro freeholders were "exceptional men . . . who have had unusual opportunity, who have been helped by [white] patrons, who have been aided by members of their own families in the North or in cities, or who have escaped the wretched crop system by some sudden rise in the price of cotton, which did not enable the landlord to take the whole economic advantage."

However, DuBois was acutely aware of the dangers of such summary statements. He knew that, of all the southern states, only Georgia had consistently kept taxation records by race. DuBois and other students of rural Negroes were also cognizant of the variables of inflation and deflation in determining the nature and value of real holdings, and of the inherent difficulties of defining "farm." Many rural plots,

Progressivism in Black   163

for example, lay on the outskirts of urban centers and towns
and were not principal sources of income to their city-
employed owners. These factors, along with topographical,
economic, and legal differences within the southern region,
made an exact measurement next to impossible. However,
the census bureau's 1900 and 1910 compilations, DuBois's
systematic study of Georgia, isolated county studies, and the
periodical literature of the era—yield enough dependable
data, analysis, and vivid impressions to formulate an overview and some educated guesswork.

Georgia's custom of taxation record-keeping by race was
particularly fortuitous. At the turn of the century, the "Empire State of the South" had a larger total black population
than any other state, and Georgia's regional variety made it
almost a model for the whole South. The northeastern
Savannah River counties, the home of the state's earliest
black laborers, had experienced soil depletion and economic
change comparable to the tidewater regions of the Upper
South. Central and West Georgia had been the eastern
center of the antebellum slave and cotton belt and had
maintained overwhelmingly black populations into the twentieth century. Hilly northern and swampy southeastern Georgia were infertile white areas, with relatively few Negroes.
Surveying counties in all these districts in the late 1890s,
DuBois published his findings in a federal Bureau of Labor
Bulletin in 1901.

DuBois found that Georgia blacks had been acquiring
land steadily since the war, with the greatest gains after
1880. In 1875, they owned about 400,000 acres; fifteen years
later, more than a million. Depressions—especially the mid-
1890s—caused setbacks to both races, but black farmers
rapidly recovered owned land in the late-1890s, thereby
compensating for their previous losses and usually exceeding
white farmers' land recoveries. Following the color line to
central Georgia's Pulaski County in 1907, white journalist
Ray Stannard Baker uncovered local statistics which indicated remarkable increases in black acreage during the

second half of the 1880s: from about 7,000 in 1885 to nearly 12,300 in 1890. By way of explanation Baker offered stories of extraordinary young men such as Robert Polhill and Ben and Charles Gordon who had been diligent and thrifty, pulling themselves upward into large proprietorships. Baker's Pulaski figures agree with DuBois's compilations, but the remainder of the black sociologist's county figures reveals no trend of remarkable increases or declines within any five-year period that were not explainable by economic conditions which also affected whites. Blacks and whites alike lost titles to land in the mid-1890s; yet, apparently more Negroes than whites *remained* in agriculture instead of moving to towns and some of them became new landowners.

In fifty-six "typical" Georgia counties which DuBois studied in depth, black owners usually occupied small parcels of land:

SIZES OF BLACK-OWNED FARMS IN 56 TYPICAL GEORGIA COUNTIES, 1899

Classified Size in Acres	Percent of Total Black Owners
Under 10	30.53
10-39	27.00
40-99	21.85
100-199	12.85
200-499	6.89
500+	0.93

Clearly, 30.53 percent of the "farms" were actually large gardens, usually near towns where their owners often earned part of their incomes outside of agriculture. About half (49 percent) measured between ten and a hundred acres. The few great planters were scattered across the state. In all 56 of DuBois's typical counties 75 men owned more than 500 acres of land each.

The extraordinary men and advances in small farm ownership should not obscure the general suffering and poverty
of the cotton belt rural black. Shortly after the appearance
of his "Negro Landholders of Georgia," DuBois wrote eloquently and painfully in *The Souls of Black Folk* of Dougherty County, Georgia (surrounding the city of Albany).
Blacks there had steadily acquired land: from no acreage in
1870 to 750 in 1875, 6,500 in 1885, 9,000 in 1890, and about
10,000 in 1900. One-hundred and eighty-five blacks owned
land some time in the last quarter of the century; there were
only 44 in 1890 and, of the 100 owners in 1898, half had
made their purchases since the Panic of 1893. Two families
owned more than 1,000 acres each, but half of the proprietors
owned fewer than 40 acres apiece. The most stunning
statistic—and the simplest to appreciate—is that the 100
landowners of 1898 were but 6 percent of the black population of Dougherty County. The owners lived the precarious
existence of one-crop commercial farmers. However, the
great mass of people in this black belt county dwelt in the
squalor, ignorance, and despondency that was the particular
lot of the landless. In some rural communities in the Louisiana delta country, blacks had apparently not yet acquired
a single acre by 1900.[5]

Outside the cotton states—where the effects of single-
staple agriculture, the rural credit drought, and white repression were not so severe—country blacks fared better and
became proprietors more easily. This is apparent not only
in the federal census statistics but in local studies conducted
around 1900.

Lancaster County, Virginia, located on the Chesapeake
Bay between the Potomac and Rappahannock rivers, is a
case in point. Lancaster was one of the oldest counties in the
nation and, by the late nineteenth century, it had evolved
from a tobacco-slave culture to a region of small, diversified
farms—83 percent of which were owner-operated in 1900.
The adult male population was almost evenly divided be-

tween the two races; blacks owned 12 percent of the county's land, 13 percent of assessed realty, and 17 percent of the assessed personal property. The percentage of black adult male freeholders is not available, but a sociologist who toured Lancaster in 1900 reported that the 10,000 to 15,000 black-owned acres had been gradually acquired and were well distributed in small farms among 1,161 adult men.

Gloucester County, Virginia, on the Chesapeake below Lancaster, yielded comparable statistics when Booker T. Washington surveyed local conditions around 1905. In Gloucester, black school teachers, trained at the nearby Hampton Institute, had led the way in educational uplift and land acquisition. School terms had been extended to about six months—this improvement based partly on enhanced black property holding and assessed realty. Gloucester County Negroes were about half the total population and had accumulated one sixth of the county's total property, most of which was in small yeoman farms, ten to a hundred acres.

Montgomery County, Maryland, in the Blue Ridge foothills northwest of Washington, was another old tobacco-slave area which had made the transition to diversified freehold farming. Eighty-four percent of the county's farms were owner-operated; only about 7 percent were sharecropped. Blacks comprised about one-fourth of the total population and included many freeholders. Montgomery's chief interest, however, lies in its Sandy Spring community. An 1898 study of blacks in Montgomery's Sandy Spring community—a colonial era Quaker settlement where many blacks had been free since the 1770s—showed considerable advances in property acquisition by both the old-free blacks, 61.4 percent of whom owned land, and those not freed until 1865, 43.1 percent of whom had become proprietors.

Perhaps the best-studied area outside DuBois's Georgia was Albemarle County, Virginia. Around 1914 Samuel T. Bitting, a white rural economist and long-time resident observer of the Charlottesville-Albemarle district, conducted a thorough investigation of local Negro landholders. Bitting's work is of special value not only for his statistical accumulations but for his personal observations and educated guesses regarding the meaning of his figures.

Albemarle lies in the geographical center of the Old Dominion; its rural economy and population were representative of the commonwealth and nearby states. Tobacco was still an important staple in the flatter eastern half of the county, which had once been plantation-slavery territory; the Blue Ridge foothills of the western part of the county remained the realm of smaller, diversified, predominantly white, farmers. From 1880 to 1910, the black population declined both absolutely and relatively; from 16,659 to 9,673 or from 51 percent to 32.4 percent of the county total. However, from 1900 to 1910, the number of black farmers declined 2.4 percent less rapidly than the black population; nearly the opposite relationship was true of whites: the white population grew by 11.3 percent, but white farmers increased by only 6.8 percent. Bitting's personal observations supported the statistical indications that, as many whites drifted into Charlottesville and other cities for employment, proportionately more blacks remained in the country and took some of the agricultural places of the more mobile whites. Although DuBois did not proffer a comparable guess for Georgia during this same period, his figures lead one to the same conclusion.

Relatively good economic conditions—and perhaps the white exodus from the country—facilitated an increasing rate of black proprietorship. Bitting believed that blacks began to buy land during a rural real estate "boom" during the 1880s. By 1910, there were 637 farmers among 1,554 black property owners and very few tenants. Indeed, of Albemarle's 408 tenants in 1910, 364 were white. Several black farmers tilled units of several hundreds of acres, but most Negro-owned property was in large vegetable gardens and small family farms. However, the blacks' land was more valuable per acre than the whites' holdings, which were generally larger units that were partly forested and unimproved.

Bitting's picture of Albemarle County compares well with existing statistical information on the whole of Virginia. The state's black population declined somewhat in relation to whites; yet, the blacks' acreage and assessed real value increased. Hampton Institute's *Southern Workman* reported that in 1892 black Virginians (41 percent of the population) owned 2.75 percent of the state's acreage assessed for taxation; in 1898 blacks were but 37 percent of the population and owned 3.23 percent of the rural acreage. (The contrary was true in Virginia cities where black property declined relatively; already, perhaps, the pressure of white militancy and urban segregation was upon them.) In 1890, 26 out of 1,000 Negroes owned unencumbered Virginia farms—one third of the white figure; by 1900, this number had grown to 42 out of 1,000—one half the current white proportion. A statistician writing in *Science* estimated that the rate of unencumbered farm acquisition among Virginia blacks during 1891-1903 was 40 percent faster than during 1865-1890. Making allowance for his erroneous assumption that blacks owned nothing before the war, it would appear obvious that black land acquisition of boom proportions was indeed in progress. Using federal census statistics, Bitting showed that during 1900-1910, Virginia Negro-owned farms increased by 21.3 percent; in 1910, fully 67 percent of the state's black farmers were owners. Virginia was, in the *Southern Workman's* expression, the "banner state."

From the maze of 1900 and 1910 census reports and the incomplete picture puzzle of the preceding decades, it seems fair to conclude that southern blacks were making gains on the land. There still remains the problem of accounting for this phenomenon.[6]

A partial explanation may lie in population growth rates. When W. E. B. DuBois toured Georgia's black belt and the countryside around Atlanta in the late 1890s he was most impressed by his perception that blacks seemed to be marrying later and raising smaller families. The 1910 census verified his prediction that the black population rate was declining.

In the 1890s, 1.3 million blacks were born; between 1900 and 1910, 300,000 fewer births were recorded, a decline in the black population growth rate of more than 6 percent. Blacks' collective decision to reduce family sizes—a decision perhaps made for many by poverty itself—must have freed many younger men to accumulate the small plots which show up in great numbers on statistical charts.

The greater movement of whites to cities before 1915 was complementary to this black demographic trend. Even though many blacks did migrate to southern cities before World War I, their exclusion from the textile factories and other urban jobs had the effect of keeping most of them in agriculture. At the same time, the white rural exodus helped create opportunity in the country for ambitious blacks.

A most important factor in this mini-rise of Negro freeholders was human initiative, a rural version of that same self-help doctrine of the towns and cities which flourished under the spokesmanship of Booker T. Washington. As freedmen became resigned to their abandonment by the federal government and the Republican party, Washington and hundreds of less well known leaders across the South inculcated middle class acquisitive values and preached the homey virtues of country living, manual labor, and proprietorship. In a very real sense, Washington and his coadjutors represented a rural progressive movement parallel to the country life movement and the business farming enthusiasm among the whites. Washingtonian "industrial education" always included agricultural training; Booker T. Washington himself was intuitively a profound agrarian who was deeply suspicious of cities: "Just as often as I can when I am at home, I like to get my hoe and dig in my garden, to come into contact with real earth, or to touch my pigs and fowls." Continuing the idyll, he managed to relate his personal sense of practicality and materialism to the wellsprings of nature: "Whenever I want new material for an address or a magazine article, I follow the plan of getting away from the town with its artificial surroundings and getting back into the country, where I can sleep in a log cabin and eat the food of the farmer." He claimed to have "gotten more material in this way than . . . by reading books." "Many [people] . . . while not educated in the way that we consider education, have in reality a very high form of education—that which they have gotten out of contact with nature.[7]

To the practical Tuskegeean, the blacks' exclusion from many industrial jobs and urban trades and their herding into miserable proto-ghettos were added reasons to promote rural proprietorship and country life. "I am convinced," he wrote in 1902, "that, for many years at least, the Negro should be encouraged to own and cultivate the soil: in a word, to remain in the country districts. He is at his best in most cases when in the country—in agricultural life; he is at his worst . . . when in contact with city life."

More resigned than rhapsodic, R. R. Wright, president of Georgia State Agricultural College, declared bitterly in 1900 that "the only real 'open door' in the industrial arena for [blacks] evidently is the farm," since "the colored man is denied work in the factories." However, other leaders readily embraced country life as morally preferable, and they enthusiastically shared some whites' and Washington's conviction that the cities were polluting the great reservoir of provincial American virtue. Hardly a student body or "farmers' day" convocation at Hampton Institute escaped agrarian speakers' commandments to "keep the young and energetic men on the farm" and "stay out of the cities of Virginia and till the soil." Like Theodore Roosevelt's Country Life Commission and white rural progressives such as Poe, blacks sought to redeem rural society through increased proprietorship, improved education, and home economics.

In the early years of the century, Washington himself attempted to vitalize rural life in Macon County, Alabama (surrounding Tuskegee). Gathering from northern white philanthropists and local blacks a Rural School Improvement Fund, Washington and his Tuskegee associates stimulated physical renovation and expansion of educational facilities and the lengthening of school terms. In five years Tuskegee and Macon Negroes spent $20 thousand and a great deal of volunteer labor. Washington also solicited the services of a farm demonstration agent, founded a local agricultural paper (the *Messenger*), and enlisted the aid of teachers and ministers toward the improvement of agricultural techniques. By 1908, advertisements in "colored newspapers" in Alabama and other southern states proclaimed Macon County's eight-month schools and progressive atmosphere. Ambitious farmers arrived and local property values soared. In 1900, only 157 black farmers owned the land they tilled; in 1910, there were 507. In a total black population of 22,000 the improvement was still pathetically small—but still adequate to encourage other self-helpers.

Concurrent with his Macon County endeavors, Washington and his northern white supporters organized the Southern Improvement Company. A joint stock and philanthropic enterprise, the company purchased some 4,000 acres of farmland in Virginia, Macon County, Alabama, and other parts of the cotton South and then resold it cheaply to blacks who were former tenants. Similar but smaller projects were undertaken by the hundreds of Hampton and Tuskegee graduates who spread across the south during these years, promoting the self-help gospel. In 1892, some of them es-tablished at Calhoun (Lowndes County), Alabama a "social settlement" with a school where previously there had been three plantations "under the bondage of the lien system of crops." Organizers supervised the collective purchase and subdivision of the plantations and the sale of plots to black yeomen.

Hampton Institute graduate Thomas C. Walker, born into slavery in Gloucester County, Virginia in 1864, led a one-man moral uplift and economic betterment campaign in his home county. Leaving Hampton in the mid-1880s, Walker taught in the colored school system, saved his money, acquired a farm, and began to apply the scientific methods he learned at the Institute. He later studied law. In 1889, at age

twenty-five, "Lawyer Walker" initiated a local-option prohibition referendum and led a successful campaign among
black voters. In the same year he founded the Gloucester
Land and Brick Company. Walker's loan and land investment
association bought farm acreage and sold it to blacks, to
whom he made cheap loans available and also additional
money for home improvement. (The "brick" in the company
name represented Walker's aspiration to replace mud and
stick chimneys with brick ones.)

Walker also led local Republicans from the time of his
majority and was elected justice of the peace several times.
He attended national party conventions, campaigned vigorously for Harrison, McKinley, and Roosevelt, and was appointed Collector of Customs for the port of Rappahannock
from 1896 to 1902. Roosevelt offered him the consulate at
Guadaloupe, but Walker declined. Meanwhile, at the time
many blacks were being disfranchised, Walker was elected—
largely by whites—as a member of the county board of
supervisors, where he served long and well. Throughout
the progressive era, he was a vocal fixture at Hampton
Institute farmers' and educators' meetings and a participant
in state black organizations, frequently exhorting fellow
Negroes to study and acquire property.

R. L. Smith's career in the Southwest was similar to
Walker's. A South Carolinian, Smith emigrated to Texas in
1885 and settled in Oakland, Colorado County, where he
taught in the village's black school. Despairing at the dilapi-
dation of the school, of blacks' meager property, and the
poverty of local cotton farmers, Smith organized a Village
Improvement Society and a Farmers' Improvement Society,
with a Women's Barnyard Auxilliary. The first group rallied
volunteers for school repair and home beautification. In the
farm groups, Smith initiated cooperative wholesale purchases
of supplies and thrifty home economics, especially poultry
and egg sales for extra cash. Smith was elected as a Republican to the state legislature in 1895 and attracted considerable
attention as one of only two blacks in the 1896 session. Using

his new statewide audience, he founded the Farmers' Improvement Society of Texas. Smith instituted Masonic-like degrees of membership and Washingtonian self-help values: getting out of debt; becoming a proprietor; education in new methods; and making profits. By 1906 the Society claimed more than 9,000 members in 475 suborganizations across the state, and it had acquired land in North Texas for the establishment of an agricultural college. In another half-dozen years, the Society owned a bank and an overall factory in Waco.

At the turn of the century, formal agricultural education for blacks lagged far behind white institutions. Except for Hampton and Tuskegee private and public financial support was meager until after 1915. Nevertheless, energetic blacks—usually graduates of the older, well established colleges—founded dozens of small, struggling schools which emphasized better farming and land acquisition. Among these were the Calhoun Colored School in Alabama, which also held monthly conferences for Lowndes County farmers; the Snow Hill Normal and Industrial School (Wilcox County, Alabama, founded 1894); the Robert Hungerford Industrial School (Eatonville, Florida, founded 1899); the Slater Industrial and State Normal School at Winston-Salem, North Carolina (founded 1892); and the Port Royal (South Carolina) Agricultural School (founded 1903). At the Utica Institute in Mississippi, Principal W. H. Holtzclaw founded a company similar to Walker's Gloucester operation and bought land for reasonably priced resale to ambitious black tenants.

Most agricultural instruction took place in farmers' institutes and conferences, state and county "Negro Agricultural Fairs," and through the pages of the *Southern Workman*, Washington's *Messenger*, the *Negro Farmer* (also Tuskegee), and other journals. The annual Hampton and Tuskegee farmers' conferences, begun during the 1890s, spread during the progressive era to black schools in Savannah; Jackson, Tennessee; Utica, Mississippi; and elsewhere. State fairs for blacks flourished in both Carolinas, Georgia, Alabama, Ten-

nessee, and Kentucky. At the 1911 meeting of the American
Association of Farmers' Institute Workers, Professor P. C.
Parks of Atlanta's Clark University acquainted delegates of
the white organization with the gains of black farmers and
urged them to participate in black farmer education. Papers
read at the 1912 session indicated that white agriculture
professors had begun to circulate in the black rural community. In rural journalism, the founding of papers such as
the *Messenger* and *Negro Farmer* after the turn of the
century and the new agricultural emphasis of the older
Southern Workman indicated the trend toward rural uplift.

These educational and reform initiatives were sustained
after 1904 by a corps of black county agents. Exploiting the
practical farming pedagogy of Seaman Knapp and following
the new style of racial separation, the Rockefeller-financed
General Education Board sent the first black demonstration
agents into the Lower South in 1905. In 1907, the Board
and Knapp's Bureau dispatched John B. Pierce to Virginia
as director of demonstration work among Negro farmers.
(T. O. Sandy simultaneously undertook the organization of
the separate white program.) A graduate of both Hampton
and Tuskegee, Pierce settled in Governor William H. Mann's
home county of Nottoway and began the slow process of
teaching black neighbors scientific agriculture by demonstrating his own and others' success. Gradually, other black
agents settled in scattered Virginia counties; by 1920 Pierce—
then Special Agent for the U.S. Department of Agriculture's
States Relations Service—directed the work of 23 agents in
Virginia alone and about 44 agents in four nearby states.
By 1914, the federal government and the states employed
resourceful men such as Pierce in all the South Atlantic
states, the Gulf area, and Oklahoma. By 1930 there would
be 171 black county agents and 128 black women serving
as home demonstration agents, principally in the South.

This black version of rural progressivism was a product
of both Negro and white efforts. The emphasis of "Booker-
ism" upon self-help economics and the avoidance of protest

politics represented the pessimism and caution blacks had learned since Reconstruction. The mechanics and techniques of "business" agriculture, much of the educational funds, and the rhetoric of the country life movement came from whites. These elements, combined with great demographic and economic changes—the white exodus to cities and the lower black birth rate—encouraged and permitted increased black freeholding over parts of the South. Whether blacks would have acquired land without the rationale of "Booker-ism" and other trappings of rural progressivism seems a moot question. Based upon the published vernacular of the times, as well as federal and state-compiled statistics, educated guesswork leads us to the conclusion that—outside the black belt, where better economic and social conditions prevailed anyway—the ideology of rural reformism was significant. It spurred the better-off blacks to become still better-off. It helped catalyze a mini-rise of Negro freeholders in the Upper South (particularly Virginia), the Trans-Mississippi South, and in northern Georgia and other black belt fringe areas.

However, most rural blacks lived inside the black belt, where the repression of whites and single-staple economics were most unyielding to the benign, middle class methods of Hampton and Tuskegee. Here great gains in land occupancy were also made by blacks—but overwhelmingly as share-croppers. Tobacco and cotton country blacks also strove for proprietorship and the vitalization of their communities, but usually in vain. Most of the "advances" heralded in the early 1910s by Washington and white alarmists such as Clarence Poe were fake. Indeed, they best represent the monumentality of the southern socioeconomic dilemma a half-century after the Civil War. Here "Bookerism"—re-formism without a political base—was woefully inadequate, and change through violent revolution was not possible or feasible. Most whites were hostile to Negro aspirations—even modest material aspirations. Friendlier, more benevolent whites who shared the ideology of Washingtonian progress chose safe, token blacks such as Thomas C. Walker and

R. L. Smith for minor posts in public life; but these men hardly offered a threat of substantive change in the basic scheme of southern affairs.

The masses still awaited an alternative when, around 1915-1916, northern opportunity beckoned in the form of thousands of industrial jobs. The Great Migration began. War in Europe and its economic windfall in effect initiated what black progressives had attempted and failed to accomplish: provision of a viable escape from the bondage of peonage. Some southern blacks would continue to acquire land despite the agricultural disasters of 1920-21 and the 1930s. But now the thrust of Black History would be migration and urban settlement, rather than rural southern adaptation. Such was the process of trial, hope, and frustration in Dixie that ultimately generated the "New Negro"—an impatient creature who turned his back on the South, often only to find equally insuperable barriers in a new environment.

EPILOGUE: THE END OF RACE

In those days in the South you didn't admit that there was a race problem and therefore you didn't talk about it.

WILL W. ALEXANDER

In my opinion, the great majority of Southerners after the 1830s had no more 'guilt complex' concerning the evil nature of Southern slavery than I and my classmates at the University of North Carolina in the 1920s (we the young liberals!) had in regard to segregation of Negroes.

CLEMENT EATON

Segregation, which was an ordinary fact of life for me, is devastatingly effective in accomplishing something that it was only peripherally designed to do: it prevents the awareness even of the existence of another race.

WILLIAM STYRON

OF course, race continued to play an important role in the South during the 1920s and after—but there were some important changes. The region now merely shared the bad publicity of brutality and repression with the North. And, if Wilbur J. Cash's "savage ideal" best expressed the white South's baser tribal ethos, now there was open acknowledgment that the Yankee was a bigot, too. More than half the urban race riots in the terrible "red summer" of 1919 occurred outside the South. Chicago's was worst of all. Furthermore, if Atlanta was imperial headquarters for the second Ku Klux Klan (founded in 1915), the public acknowledged Ohio as having more Klan members than any other state. Only Indiana's and Oklahoma's state governments were Klan-controlled—while in some southern states, such as Virginia, North Carolina, and Louisiana, the white knights were pathetically weak. Northern and western Klansmen were preoccupied with Jews, Catholics, the foreign-born, and the politically radical. But the Negro, now present in increasingly larger numbers in nonsouthern cities, held an important place, too, in the Yankee's pantheon of fearful intruders. In short, the 1920s witnessed the first revelations of a great truth which would only be generally accepted in the late-1960s: that the white South has never held a monopoly on racism.[1]

Yet, recognition of national sin in the late 1960s was virtually absent in the 1920s. Segregation did its job well. Discounting the aberrations of 1919, lynchings and burnings declined after the turn of the century and the imposition of the southern race settlement. Southern reformers claimed a direct relationship between relative racial "peace" and the disfranchisement of blacks and formalized segregation. Northerners, so recently schooled during the debate over the Philippines, were inclined to accept southern lessons. Customary segregation was already common in the North; because of the wartime black migration, Yankees now defended their color line vigorously, occasionally adopting southern *de jure* schemes of neighborhood and other separation.

However, the most important product of the progressive reform of segregation was the insidious one referred to by Clement Eaton and William Styron. As existing separation in the schools and churches grew to envelop nearly every aspect of daily life, communications—except for the most controlled employer-employee sort—were cut off. More than ever before, blacks became mere shadow people to whites—existing more as spectors or a part of the landscape, than as real, human individuals. The Negro became, in the shockingly appropriate title of Ralph Ellison's novel, *The Invisible Man*. Against such nonpeople, the old styles of repression—so furious and often so personal—were not necessary. The law itself and society's institutions now accomplished the job. The question was settled and buried. Will Alexander, the gentle pastor who founded the Commission on Interracial Cooperation in 1919, was a rare southern white who recognized injustice and sought to restore the severed lines of communication. More common were the "young liberals" of Chapel Hill whom Clement Eaton recalled, whites liberated from the old preoccupation with race by the race settlement and progressive reformist attitudes.

In the claims made for segregation by southern progressive reformers lies an additional irony. The most paternalistic and humane of the white racial reformers (especially Murphy and Poe) had placed such high hopes in segregation; it would bring peace, guarantee racial integrity, and lay the basis for the moral and material development of both races. Yet, segregation and the moral principles underlying paternalism were incompatible. The black human beings, whose propinquity before 1900 whites both enjoyed and feared, ceased being quite human to whites after a generation of separation. With much daily personal contact now impossible, the opportunity for charity and guidance was diminished. Murphy did not survive to witness the age of segregation, but one wonders if other humane paternalists understood the consequences of their race settlement, if they were satisfied with their changed roles in the decades after World War I, and if they were able and content to "help the darkies" from the impersonal distance required by the new racial arrangement. Other whites, however, were no doubt contented with the results of racial reform in the progressive years. Segregation brought more than three decades of relative calm and freed the whites to continue the building of the public service state, begun also as part of progressive reform.

The growth of public services based upon sound "business" practices, as well as humanitarian programs, continued into the 1920s. There was no "end" imposed by the war, Republicans in Washington, or the Age of Ballyhoo. The administrative terms of many southern governors concerned with broadened and efficient services encompassed the war years and the transition to the new decade. They helped prepare the way for triumphant "business progressive" state regimes during the 1920s: Harry Byrd's in Virginia, Cameron Morrison's in North Carolina, Austin Peay's in Tennessee, Bibb Graves's in Alabama—and—the most important of all—Huey Long's in Louisiana. Better schools—primarily for whites—better roads, and more efficiently operated prisons and other state institutions were characteristic issues. All originated in the progressive years.

Progressive reformers' campaigns before the war became customary services after the war. The county and home demonstration agent systems flourished in the '20s and fostered further demands for assistance to farm people from government. Free high schools, arterial highways (not to mention Prohibition enforcement agencies) were everywhere. Southern counties continued to outdistance the rest of the nation in public health agencies. And campaigns against hookworm, pellagra, and malaria, the cures for which were all prescribed in the progressive years, finally met some successes.

To be sure, there were difficult years ahead. Youth black and white left the farms despite Clarence Poe's and others' exhortations. The nagging dilemmas of agriculture in the one-crop areas would not yield to moderate "business" type reforms. And growing cities such as Atlanta, Memphis, New Orleans, and Dallas spawned new problems much like the urban North's old ones. However, the basis for the region's emergence from the travails of the late nineteenth century were finally established. Despite many continuing frustrations, one could confidently predict, by the ending of World War I, a new era of well-being for the South. It was a dawning. To most whites, at least, the dark whirlwind within their ambitious reforms was not as apparent as it would be half a century later—at reaping time.

ACKNOWLEDGMENTS

EXTENDED research tours in the South and a wonderful summer devoted entirely to this project were made possible by generous grants of money from the American Philosophical Society in Philadelphia and from Miami University; without these the book would have been delayed by years. Like all scholars I am indebted, too, to knowledgable and friendly librarians, especially at the Library of Congress, the principal university libraries in Virginia, Kentucky, and both Carolinas, the historical society libraries of Kentucky, North and South Carolina, and at the State Department of Archives and History in Raleigh. I am particularly grateful for the marvelous Southern Historical Collection at the University of North Carolina's Wilson Library. There the richest manuscript sources from throughout the region are preserved; and there courtesy, efficiency, and a fine working atmosphere prevail. My debt to previous scholars in this field (especially C. Vann Woodward) is indicated in the notes and bibliography at the end of the book. My students helped sharpen my conceptualization of reform in the progressive era. However, if this book possesses much conceptual rigor and clarity, it is owed largely to Paul K. Conkin's tough-minded editorship. Of· course, the book's weaknesses are entirely mine. Part of Chapter VI appeared previously, in a somewhat different form, in the *South*

Atlantic Quarterly (Vol. LXVIII, No. 1, Winter 1969); permission to republish is appreciated.

This book is dedicated to two women whose examples of courage, humor, and toleration are difficult to emulate.

                                                          J.T.K.

Oxford, Ohio
April, 1971

NOTES AND BIBLIOGRAPHY

PROLOGUE

[1]Some of the important studies of progressivism, national and southern, are George Mowry, *The California Progressives* (Berkeley and Los Angeles: University of California Press, 1948); Mowry's *Theodore Roosevelt and the Progressive Movement, 1901-1916* (New York: Harper and Row, 1958); Richard Hofstadter, *The Age of Reform: From Bryan to FDR* (New York: Alfred A. Knopf, 1955); Arthur S. Link, "The South and the Democratic Campaign of 1912," (University of North Carolina Ph.D. dissertation, 1945); and Link's *Woodrow Wilson and the Progressive Era, 1910-1917* (New York: Harper and Row, 1954), and his *Wilson: The Road to the White House* (Princeton: Princeton University Press, 1947); C. Vann Woodward, *Origins of the New South, 1877-1913* (Baton Rouge: Louisiana State University Press, 1951), latter chapters; George B. Tindall, *The Emergence of the New South, 1913-1945* (Baton Rouge: Louisiana State University Press, 1969), Chapter I; Robert H. Wiebe, *The Search for Order, 1877-1920* (New York: Hill and Wang, 1967); Samuel Haber, *Efficiency and Uplift: Scientific Management and Progressivism* (Chi-cago: University of Chicago Press, 1964); Samuel P. Hays, *Conservation and the Gospel of Efficiency* (Chicago: University of Chicago Press, 1959); Raymond H. Pulley, *Old Virginia Restored: An Interpretation of the Progressive Impulse, 1870-1930* (Charlottesville: University Press of Virginia, 1968). Other important southern state studies and biographies are cited below.

[2]Hofstadter first offered a dichotomous interpretation of progressivism in *The Age of Reform*, especially page 133. More recently, perceptive dichotomous portraits have been drawn by Paul W. Glad, *The Trumpet Soundeth: William Jennings Bryan and His Democracy, 1896-1912* (Lincoln: University of Nebraska Press, 1960), pp. 110-14; John Braeman, "Seven Progressives," *Business History Review*, XXXV (Winter, 1961), 581-92; Samuel P. Hays, "New Interpretations of American Political History, 1880-1920," a paper read at the American Historical Association convention, December, 1961; and Wiebe, *Search for Order*, Chapters IV through VII.

[3]Within the great body of literature on American white racial attitudes, three excellent and useful sources are: Guion Griffis Johnson,

185

"The Ideology of White Supremacy, 1876-1910," in Fletcher M. Green, ed., *Essays in Southern History* (Chapel Hill: University of North Carolina Press, 1949), pp. 124-56; Winthrop D. Jordan, *White Over Black: American Attitudes Toward the Negro, 1550-1812* (Chapel Hill: University of North Carolina Press, 1968); and I. A. Newby, *Jim Crow's Defense: Anti-Negro Thought in America, 1900-1930* (Berkeley and Los Angeles: University of California Press, 1965). Also, although I disagree with parts of Lawrence J. Friedman's *The White Savage: Racial Fantasies in the Postbellum South* (Englewood Cliffs, N.J.: Prentice-Hall, 1970), his perceptions of late-nineteenth century white racial ideology in the South are most valuable and complement in some ways my own work.

I: OUT OF THE DARK AGES

[1]On the interrelated subjects of rural distress, class politics in the late nineteenth century, and the coming of disfranchisement and *de jure* Jim Crow in the various states, see the following sources, which are listed here in the approximate order that they are employed in the chapter: Emory Q. Hawk, *Economic History of the South* (New York: Henry Holt and Company, 1934); Fred A. Shannon, *The Farmers' Last Frontier, 1860-1897* (New York: Henry Holt and Company, 1945); Theodore Saloutos, *Farmer Movements in the South, 1865-1933* (Berkeley and Los Angeles: University of California Press, 1960), especially early chapters. My basic concepts and definitions are C. Vann Woodward's; see his classic *Origins of the New South,*

especially pp. 72-204. See also Woodward's *Tom Watson, Agrarian Rebel* (New York: Oxford University Press, 1938), pp. 259-301, which is still the best work on southern populism; and another study sympathetic to the rural protesters, Normal Pollack, *The Populist Response to Industrial America* (New York: W. W. Norton and Company, 1962). One must take into account, however, the work of two young scholars who question, among other things, the degree of black-white cooperation in the Populist movement suggested by Woodward: Robert Saunders, "Southern Populists and the Negro, 1893-1895," *Journal of Negro History*, LIV (July, 1969), 240-61; and Friedman, *The White Savage*, Chapter 5. V. O. Key's irreplaceable *Southern Politics, In State and Nation* (New York: Alfred A. Knopf, 1949), emphasizes the forceful *de facto* disfranchisement of southern Negroes prior to the constitutional revisions. For the position of the Republican party see Stanley P. Hirshon, *Farewell to the Bloody Shirt. Northern Republicans and the Southern Negro, 1877-1893* (Bloomington: Indiana University Press, 1962); and Vincent P. DeSantis, *Republicans Face the Southern Question: The New Departure Years 1877-1897* (Baltimore: Johns Hopkins Press, 1959).

On the states see Helen Edmonds, *The Negro and Fusion Politics in North Carolina* (Chapel Hill: University of North Carolina Press, 1951); Frenise A. Logan, *The Negro in North Carolina, 1876-1894* (Chapel Hill: University of North Carolina Press, 1964), 14-17; Vernon L. Wharton's *The Negro in Mississippi,* ond half (this book broke the path for Woodward); Albert D. Kirwan, *Revolt of the Rednecks: Mississippi Politics, 1875-1925* (New York: Harper and Row, 1965 ed.), pp. 18-215; Francis Butler Simkins, *Pitchfork Ben Tillman, South Carolinian* (Baton Rouge: Louisiana State University Press, 1944), pp. 285-309; George B. Tindall, *South Carolina Negroes, 1877-1895* (Chapel Hill: University of North Carolina Press, 1952); Oliver H. Orr, *Charles B. Aycock* (Chapel Hill: University of North Carolina Press, 1961), pp. 83-188; Sheldon Hackney, *From Populism to Progressivism in Alabama* (Princeton: Princeton University Press, 1969), pp. 181-217, 243; Nelson Blake, *William Mahone of Virginia: Soldier and Political Insurgent* (Richmond: Dietz Press, 1935); Charles E. Wynes, *Race Relations in Virginia, 1870-1902* (Charlottesville: University of Virginia Press, 1961); Hermon L. Horn, "The Democratic Party in Virginia since 1890" (Duke Ph.D. dissertation, 1949), is a standard, reliable study which should have been published (see here pp. 180-81, 360-61, 369); also excellent is James A. Bear, "Thomas Staples Martin: A Study in Virginia Politics, 1883-1896" (University of Virginia master's thesis, 1952), pp. 146-47, 357-58; Allen W. Moger, *Virginia: Bourbonism to Byrd, 1870-1925* (Charlottesville: University Press of Virginia, 1968) is a useful political survey of the period. Also on Virginia see William Larsen's sympathetic *Montague of Virginia: The Making of a Southern Progressive* (Baton Rouge: Louisiana State University Press, 1965); Pulley's *Old Virginia Restored*, which finds reformism essentially reactionary; and Jack Temple Kirby,

Westmoreland Davis: Virginia Planter-Politician, 1859-1942 (Charlottesville: University Press of Virginia, 1968), Chapter III. On Georgia and Oklahoma consult Woodward's *Tom Watson*; Dewey W. Grantham's detailed *Hoke Smith and the Politics of the New South* (Baton Rouge: Louisiana State University Press, 1967 ed.), pp. 58-62; and Keith L. Bryant, Jr., "Kate Barnard, Organized Labor, and Social Justice in Oklahoma During the Progressive Era," *Journal of Southern History*, XXXV (May, 1969), 145-65.

[2]The remainder of the chapter, treating the background of American racism and segregation and the origins and development of the southern racial settlement, is based upon the following sources, listed approximately in the order employed: C. Vann Woodward's *Strange Career of Jim Crow* (2nd rev. ed.; New York: Oxford University Press, 1966), especially Chapters I-III, is the pioneer study and still basic; see also Woodward's *Origins of the New South*; Samuel R. Spencer, *Booker T. Washington and the Negro's Place in American Life* (Boston: Little Brown and Company, 1955), pp. 108-43, which sympathetically portrays Washington's policy of accommodation; Gilbert T. Stephenson, "The Segregation of White and Negro Races in Cities," *South Atlantic Quarterly*, XIII (January, 1914), 1-18, is an authoritative account by a white judge from North Carolina; and Roger L. Rice, "Residential Segregation by Law, 1910-1917," *Journal of Southern History*, XXXIV (May, 1968), 179-199.

Racism, race relations, and segregation from colonial times through Reconstruction are explored in: Jordan, *White Over Black*; August

Meier and Elliot M. Rudwick, *From Plantation to Ghetto: An Interpretive History of American Negroes* (New York: Hill and Wang, 1966), the earlier chapters; Leon F. Litwack, *North of Slavery: The Negro in the Free States, 1790-1860* (Chicago: University of Chicago Press, 1961), an excellent study; Richard C. Wade, *Slavery in the Cities: The South, 1820-1860* (New York: Oxford University Press, 1964), pp. 266-78; Joel R. Williamson, *After Slavery: The Negro in South Carolina During Reconstruction, 1861-1877* (Chapel Hill: University of North Carolina Press, 1965); Wharton, *Negro in Mississippi*; Tindall, *South Carolina Negroes*; Arthur Zilversmit, *The First Emancipation: The Abolition of Slavery in the North* (Cambridge, Mass.: Harvard University Press, 1967); Richard W. Pih, "The Negro in Cincinnati, 1802-1841" (Miami University master's thesis, 1968); Louis R. Harlan, "Desegregation in New Orleans Public Schools during Reconstruction," *American Historical Review* LXVII (April, 1962), 663-75; Emma Lou Thornbrough, *The Negro in Indiana Before 1900* (Indianapolis: Indiana Historical Society, 1957), pp. 316-47.

On the late-nineteenth century debate see: Hinton Rowan Helper, "The Negroes in Negroland," in Joel Williamson, ed., *The Origins of Segregation* (Boston: D.C. Heath and Company, 1968), pp. 55-64; George Washington Cable, "The Freedman's Case in Equity," *Century Magazine*, XXIX (January, 1885), 409-18; Arlin Turner, *George W. Cable, A Biography* (Baton Rouge: Louisiana State University Press, 1966), pp. 194-207; Friedman, *The White Savage*, Part 2; Paul M. Gaston, *The New South*

Creed: A Study in Southern Mythmaking (New York: Alfred A. Knopf, 1970), pp. 151-86. Charles Gayarré is quoted by Clement Eaton, *The Waning of the Old South Civilization, 1860-1880s* (Athens: University of Georgia Press, 1968), pp. 145-46. Lewis Harvie Blair's remarkable book was edited and introduced by Woodward and republished as *A Southern Prophesy: The Prosperity of the South Dependent Upon the Elevation of the Negro*. On Watson's racial radicalism see Woodward's *Tom Watson*, pp. 129-58; and Thomas E. Watson, "The Negro Question in the South," *Arena*, VI (September, 1892), 540-50.

Ray Stannard Baker's observations in the recently segregated South are recorded in *Following the Color Line* (New York: Harper and Row, 1963 ed.), pp. 3-108. DuBois' remarks are from *Souls of Black Folk* (Chicago: A. C. McClurg, 1903), pp. 183-84.

II: THE SOUTH VERSUS LEVIATHAN

[1]Material on rural-based mass leaders like Tillman, Blease, Watson, Vardaman, Bilbo, and Jeff Davis is from Simkins, *Pitchfork Ben Tillman*; Woodward, *Tom Watson* and *Origins of the New South*, pp. 393-94, 376-77, 291-320; Kirwan, *Revolt of the Rednecks*, latter chapters; William F. Holmes, *The White Chief: James Kimble Vardaman* (Baton Rouge: Louisiana State University Press, 1970), latter chapters; Tindall, *Emergence of the New South*, pp. 23-25; Charles Jacobsen, *The Life Story of Jeff Davis, The Story Petrel of Arkansas Politics* (Little Rock: n.p., 1925).

[2]Woodward, *Origins of the New*

South, pp. 291-320; Mowry, *Theodore Roosevelt and the Progressive Movement, passim*; John F. Stover, *The Railroads of the South, 1865-1900* (Chapel Hill: University of North Carolina Press, 1955), *passim*; Gabriel Kolko, *The Triumph of Conservatism: A Reinterpretation of American History, 1900-1916* (1963; New York: Quadrangle Books, 1967 printing), pp. 113-38.

[3]On Texas and southwestern radicalism see Robert C. Cotner, *James Stephen Hogg, A Biography* (Austin: University of Texas Press, 1959), pp. 215-446; Tindall, *Emergence of the New South*, pp. 26-29; David A. Shannon, *The Socialist Party of America, A History* (Chicago: Quadrangle Books, 1967), pp. 34-36.

[4]On murder, mayhem, and organized violence see David D. Wallace, *South Carolina, A Short History, 1520-1948* (Chapel Hill: University of North Carolina Press, 1951), p. 651; Paul E. Isaac, *Prohibition & Politics: Turbulent Decades in Tennessee, 1885-1920* (Knoxville: University of Tennessee Press, 1965), pp. 182-231; Woodward, *Origins of the New South*, pp. 391-92, 158-60; 374-78; Thomas D. Clark, *A History of Kentucky* (Lexington: University of Kentucky Press, 1957), pp. 355, 605-23; Paul J. Vanderwood, *Night Riders of Reelfoot Lake* (Memphis: Memphis State University Press, 1969); William F. Holmes, "Whitecapping: Agrarian Violence in Mississippi, 1902-1906," *Journal of Southern History*, XXXV (May, 1969), 165-85; Woodward, *Tom Watson*, latter chapters; Gerald M. Capers, "The Rural Lag on Southern Cities," *Mississippi Quarterly*, XLIII (Fall, 1968), 253-61; W. J. Cash, *The Mind of the South* (New York:

Alfred A. Knopf, 1941), *passim*; John Hope Franklin, *The Militant South, 1800-1860* (Cambridge: Harvard University Press, 1956); Jordan, *White Over Black*; Sheldon Hackney, "Southern Violence," in Hugh Davis Graham and Ted Robert Greer, eds., *A History of Violence in America; A Report to the National Commission on the Causes and Prevention of Violence* (New York: The New York Times, 1969), pp. 505-27; John G. Miller, *The Black Patch War* (Lexington: University of Kentucky Press, 1936); James O. Nall, *The Tobacco Night Riders of Kentucky and Tennessee, 1905-1909* (Lexington: University of Kentucky Press, 1939); Saloutos, *Farmer Movements in the South*, pp. 231-34.

[5]Josephus Daniels, *Editor in Politics* (Chapel Hill: University of North Carolina Press, 1941), pp. 164, 283-312, 618-19, and *passim*; Woodward, *Origins of the New South*, pp. 381-84; Joseph F. Steelman, "The Progressive Era in North Carolina, 1884-1917" (University of North Carolina Ph.D. dissertation, 1954), pp. 547-59, 361, 576-80. Steelman's is an exhaustive study, a goldmine for scholars, but apparently too lengthy for publication. Also: Aubrey Lee Brooks, *Walter Clark: Fighting Judge* (Chapel Hill; University of North Carolina Press, 1944); see also the materials on the Comer v. L & N struggle in the Braxton Bragg Comer Papers, University of North Carolina Library.

[6]The section on Edward J. Justice is based upon Steelman, "Progressive Era in North Carolina," quotation p. 307; and "Extracts from a Speech of E. J. Justice, At a Banquet in Los Angeles on Jackson Day, January 8, 1916," a pamphlet, and Jus-

tice's draft of an article for the *Raleigh News and Observer* (ca. January 1911), both in the Justice Papers, University of North Carolina Library.

[7]Biographical and political material concerning the variety of traditional reform and the nature of southern state "machines" is based upon Pulley, *Old Virginia Restored*, pp. 111-51; Larsen, *Montague of Virginia;* Orr, *Aycock;* Samuel Proctor, *Napoleon Bonaparte Broward, Florida's Fighting Democrat* (Gainesville: University of Florida Press, 1950); Duncan Clinch Heyward Account Books, 1887-1913, South Caroliniana Library, University of South Carolina; Margaret Ola Spigner, "The Public Life of D. C. Heyward, 1903-1907, (University of South Carolina master's thesis, 1951); Tindall, *Emergence of the New South,* pp. 21-27; Tucker political correspondence, 1903-1917, and copy of Tulane Law School guest lecture, January, 1917, in Henry St. George Tucker Papers, University of North Carolina Library; Ronald E. Shibley, "G. Walter Mapp: Politics and Prohibition in Virginia, 1893-1941," (University of Virginia master's thesis, 1966); Kirby, *Westmoreland Davis,* pp. 93-94; Henry C. Ferrell, "Claude A. Swanson of Virginia," (University of Virginia Ph.D. dissertation, 1964); Henry C. Ferrell, "Prohibition, Reform, and Politics in Virginia, 1895-1916," in *Studies in the History of the South, 1875-1922* (Greenville, N.C.: East Carolina University, 1966), III, 175-242. Jack T. Kirby, "The Democratic Organization and its Challenges, 1899-1922," *Virginia Social Science Journal,* I (1966), 35-45; Steelman, "Progressive Era in North Carolina," p. 716 and *passim.*

III: UP WITH HUMANITY—AND EXPERTS

[1]On reform in southern cities and the movements for efficiency in governments see Arthur S. Link, "The South and the Democratic Campaign of 1912," 153-54 (on New Orleans); Jean M. Gordon to John M. Parker, January 28, 1911, and other Gordon-Parker correspondence in John M. Parker Papers, University of North Carolina Library; John Joseph Duffy, "Charleston Politics in the Progressive Era," (University of South Carolina Ph.D. dissertation, 1963); Civic Club of Charleston, S.C., *Yearbook, 1910-1911* and *1941,* in Civil Club Papers, South Carolina Historical Society, Charleston; Eric F. Goldman, *Charles J. Bonaparte, Patrician Reformer, His Earlier Career* (Baltimore: Johns Hopkins Press, 1943); James B. Crooks, *Politics and Progress: The Rise of Urban Progressivism in Baltimore, 1895 to 1911* (Baltimore: John Hopkins Press, 1968); Lloyd C. Taylor, Jr., "Lila Meade Valentine: FFV Reformer," *Virginia Magazine of History and Biography,* LXX (October, 1962), 471-87; Pulley, *Old Virginia Restored,* pp. 135-37; also Lila M. Valentine folder, Valentine Museum, Richmond; William D. Miller, *Mr. Crump of Memphis* (Baton Rouge: Louisiana State University Press, 1964), pp. 2-23, 28-116; Wiebe, *Search for Order,* pp. 111-63; Woodward, *Origins of the New South,* pp. 388-89; Steelman, "Progressive Era in North Carolina," p. 468; Kirby, *Westmoreland Davis,* pp. 34-35, 79-82 and *passim;* Tindall, *Emergence of the New South,* pp. 22-23.

[2]The discussion of the social welfare, women's reform, and public

service movements is based upon Lyda Gordon Shivers, "The Social Welfare Movement in the South: A Study in Regional Culture and Social Organization," (University of North Carolina Ph.D. dissertation, 1935), pp. 50-62, 91-94, 154-66; Virginia Wooten Gulledge, *The North Carolina Conference for Social Service: A Study of Its Development and Methods* (n.p., 1942); Anne Firor Scott, *The Southern Lady: From Pedestal to Politics, 1830-1930* (Chicago: University of Chicago Press, 1970), pp. 113-17, 143-44; Jane Zimmerman, "The Penal Reform Movement in the South During the Progressive Era, 1890-1917," *Journal of Southern History*, XXVII (May, 1962), 462-88; Kirby, *Westmoreland Davis*, 98-103; Tindall, *Emergence of the New South*, pp. 24-25, 276-80; Steelman, "Progressive Era in North Carolina," pp. 642-50; and on Walter Hines Page's role in the antihookworm campaign see Burton J. Hendrick, *The Training of an American: The Earlier Life and Letters of Walter Hines Page* (New York: Doubleday, 1928), II, 257.

[3]This and the following material on the national impact of southern reformism are drawn largely from valuable unpublished sources: Anne Firor Scott, "The Southern Progressive in National Politics, 1906-1916," (Radcliffe Ph.D. dissertation, 1957); Edward M. Silbert, "Support for Reform Among Congressional Democrats, 1899-1913," (University of Florida Ph.D. dissertation, 1966); John W. Davidson, "The Response of the South to Woodrow Wilson's New Freedom, 1912-14," (Yale Ph.D. dissertation, 1953). See also Glad, *Trumpet Soundeth*, pp. 81-172: Woodward. *Origins of the New*

South, pp. 470-81; Link, *Woodrow Wilson and the Progressive Era;* Wiebe, *Search for Order*, pp. 164-95. The Texas congressman is quoted by Tindall, *Emergence of the New South*, p. 14; see also pp. 7-17. Nancy J. Weiss chronicles the rise of bureaucratic segregation in "The Negro and the New Freedom: Fighting Wilsonian Segregation," *Political Science Quarterly*, LXXXIV (March, 1968), 61-79.

IV: REFORM AND MASTERY: A MEDLEY OF MINISTERS

[1]On "social control" as an early twentieth century concept see Wiebe, *Search for Order,* pp. 133-63; Hofstadter, *The Age of Reform,* pp. 133-73; Christopher Lasch, *The New American Radicalism, 1889-1963: The Intellectual as a Social Type* (New York: Alfred A. Knopf, 1965), 13-15; Edward A. Ross, *Social Control: A Survey of the Foundations of Order* (New York: Macmillan Company, 1901); on earlier American social control reformisnt see David B. Davis, ed., *Ante Bellum Reform* (New York: Harper and Row, 1968).

[2]Pertinent sources on the power and nature of Old South and Confederate mythology are Gaston, *New South Creed,* pp. 1-14, 167-77 and *passim;* William R. Taylor, *Cavalier and Yankee: The Old South and the Dual Origins of American Character* (New York: George Braziller, 1956). In *Old Virginia Restored,* Raymond Pulley eloquently describes the power of the "Old Virginia Mystique" over early twentieth century progressive reformers. Important uncritical apostrophes to the old regime are U. B. Phillips, *Amer-*

ican Negro Slavery (New York: D. Appleton and Company 1918); Thomas Nelson Page, "Marse Chan," *Harper's Magazine,* XXXIV (1884); and Edgar Gardner Murphy's "The Task of the Leader," *Sewanee Review* XXIII (1907), 3-14, a complete, corrected draft of which is to be found in the Murphy Papers, University of North Carolina Library.

[3]On Murphy's life see Hugh C. Bailey's competently researched and very sympathetic biography, *Edgar Gardner Murphy, Gentle Progressive* (Coral Cables, Fla.: University of Miami Press, 1968), especially pp. 1-20; and Daniel Levine, *Varieties of Reform Thought* (Madison: State Historical Society of Wisconsin, 1964), pp. 78-94. On the child labor movement see Walter I. Trattner, *Crusade for the Children: A History of the National Child Labor Committee and Child Labor Reform in America* (Chicago: Quadrangle, 1970).

[4]Murphy, *The Basis of Ascendancy* (New York: Longmans and Company, 1910), pp. 3-12. Excellent references for the persistent demonology of Reconstruction are Kenneth M. Stampp, *The Era of Reconstruction, 1865-1877* (New York: Alfred A. Knopf, 1965), pp. 3-23; Staughton Lynd, ed.), *Reconstruction* (New York: Harper and Row, 1967); W. E. B. DuBois, *Black Reconstruction in America, 1860-1880* (New York: World Publishers, 1935), last chapter; Gaston, *New South Creed,* pp. 168-88. For Henry Grady's diplomatic use of Reconstruction see Joel Chandler Harris, ed., *Life and Speeches of Henry W. Grady* (New York: Cassell Publishers, 1890). Among the many Murphy references to Reconstruction

see his Philadelphia speech on the eve of the Montgomery race conference, "The White Man and The Negro at the South, March 8, 1900," the draft in the Murphy Papers. For Yankee endorsements of his *Present South* see the Macmillan Company advertisement, *ibid.*

[5]The foregoing representation of Murphy's ideas is based upon his "Task of the Leader," *The Present South* (New York: Macmillan Company, 1904), and *The Basis of Ascendancy.* Reference to the origins of "bourbon" and "aristocrat" is from Woodward, *Origins of the New South,* p. 75.

[6]The discussion of Murphy and the Beveridge bill and his racial motivation for opposition is based upon: Murphy, *Present South,* 126-34; Murphy to the editor of the *New York Evening Post,* May 2, 1903, in Murphy Papers; Murphy "Shall the Fourteenth Amendment Be Enforced?" *North American Review,* CLXXX (January, 1905), pp. 109-33; Murphy to A. J. McKelway, January 23, 1905, Murphy Papers; Elizabeth H. Davidson, *Child Labor Legislation in the Southern Textile States* (Chapel Hill: University of North Carolina Press, 1939); Bailey, *Murphy,* pp. 47-103; Samuel McCune Lindsay to George Foster Peabody, January 25, 1907, Murphy Papers; Murphy to editors of the *New York Evening Post,* March 9, 1907, and to *Outlook,* March 16, 1907, and to Francis G. Caffey, November 30, 1906, to Felix Adler, May 27, 1907, and to Theodore Roosevelt, February 4, 1907, *ibid.* See also copy of National Child Labor Committee resolution of November 26, 1907, and Robert W. DeForest to Murphy, January 8, 1908, and Francis G.

Caffey to Murphy, November 30, 1906, *ibid.* (Sources are listed here in order of their implementation in the text.)

[7] On McKelway's earlier career see Betty Jane Brandon, "Alexander Jeffrey McKelway: Statesman of the New Order," (Ph.D. dissertation, University of North Carolina, 1969), an exhaustively researched biography which avoids analysis; and the Alexander J. McKelway Papers, Library of Congress.

[8] The analysis of McKelway's reform career is based upon Brandon, "McKelway" and the following materials in the McKelway Papers: McKelway, "Justice, Kindness, Religion," a sermon at the 1913 meeting of the National Conference of Charities and Corrections, Seattle; McKelway, "Awakening of the South Against Child Labor," December 13, 1906 address before the 3rd annual meeting, National Child Labor Committee; McKelway, "Child Labor in its Relation to Education," (n.d.); McKelway to editor of *The Suffragist,* December, 1914; McKelway to Woodrow Wilson, October 2, 1912 and November 12, 1912; Carrie Chapman Catt to McKelway, July 17, 1917; draft of untitled speech in 1910 at Smithfield, North Carolina and other child labor materials.

[9] On McKelway and the race issue see: McKelway, "The North Carolina Revolution Justified," *Outlook,* LX (December 31, 1898), 1057-59; McKelway, "The Atlanta Riots: A Southern White Point of View," *ibid.,* LXXXIV (November 3, 1906), 557-62; Charles Crowe, "Racial Massacre at Atlanta, September 22, 1906," *Journal of Negro History,* LIV (April, 1969), 150-68; McKelway, "The Menace of Race-Degen-

eration in America" (ca. 1910), draft in McKelway Papers; McKelway to Albert S. Burleson, July 30, 1914, McKelway Papers; Brandon, "McKelway," 416-17; Hugh C. Bailey, *Liberalism in the New South; Social Reformers in the Progressive Era* (Coral Gables, Fla.: University of Miami Press, 1969), 222-26.

On the sexual basis of white racism see: Hernton, *Sex and Racism in America;* Jordan, *White Over Black;* Eldridge Cleaver, *Soul on Ice* (New York: Grove Press, 1966); and the earlier chapters of *The Autobiography of Malcolm X* (New York: Grove Press, 1965), especially pp. 56-126.

[10] Brandon, "McKelway," 287-300; McKelway quoted by Bailey, *Liberalism in the New South,* 65-66; McKelway, "Compulsory Education and Child Labor," draft of address to Georgia Sociological Society, n.d., McKelway Papers.

[11] On the subject of the Protestant clergy and reform see: Hofstadter, *Age of Reform,* 150-52; Shivers, "Social Welfare Movement in the South," 100-07; and David P. Thelen, "Social Tensions and the Origins of Progressivism," *Journal of American History,* LVI (September, 1969), 323-41, an excellent article which takes to task the older view that reformers reform because they represent a certain class or profession under special stress.

For James Cannon Jr.'s background see Richard L. Watson, ed., *Bishop Cannon's Own Story: Life As I Have Seen It, By James Cannon, Jr.* (Durham, N.C.: Duke University Press, 1955), especially Watson's long introduction and pp. 4-15, 28, 103, 145-46; Virginius Dabney, *Dry Messiah: The Life of Bishop*

Cannon (New York: Alfred A. Knopf, 1949), especially pp. 3-48; early Cannon letters in the James Cannon, Jr. Papers, Duke University Library, including his first sermon, dated 1888; Cannon, "In Defense of Decency," *Baltimore and Richmond Christian Advocate* (March 5, 1905), copy *ibid.*; Cannon, "Heresy-Hunting vs. Criminal Tolerance," *Nashville Christian Advocate* (March 8, 1907), copy *ibid.*; Cannon, "Need of Public High Schools in Virginia," *Baltimore and Richmond Christian Advocate* (January 18, 1906), copy *ibid.*; and Robert A. Hohner's "Bishop Cannon's Apprenticeship in Temperance Politics, 1901-1918," *Journal of Southern History*, XXXIV (February, 1968), 33-49.

[12]This and the succeeding narrative is largely based upon the work of Robert A. Hohner, the authority on Virginia prohibition. See his "Bishop Cannon's Apprenticeship," cited previously; his "Prohibition and Virginia Politics: William Hodges Mann versus Henry St. George Tucker, 1909," *Virginia Magazine of History and Biography*, LXXIV (January, 1966), 88-107; and his 1965 Duke dissertation, "Prohibition and Virginia Politics, 1900-1916." See also Kirby, *Westmoreland Davis*, pp. 54-58; Kirby, "The Democratic Organization and its Challenges"; and Alvin L. Hall, "The Prohibition Movement in Virginia, 1826-1916," (University of Virginia masters thesis, 1964); as well as Dabney's *Dry Messiah*, pp. 138-342; and Watson's *Cannon's Own Story*, xxviii.

V: HISTORY AND EDUCATION—
PROGRESSIVE STYLE

[1]The principal source for a dis-

cussion of the early twentieth century historians and their significance is Richard Hofstadter's excellent *The Progressive Historians: Turner, Beard, Parrington* (New York: Alfred A. Knopf, 1968). See also Harvey Wish, *The American Historian: A Social-Intellectual History of the Writing of the American Past* (New York: Oxford University Press, 1960), especially pp. 240, 248, where U. B. Phillips is quoted. Consult Phillips' *American Negro Slavery*, cited earlier; and his briefer history, *Life and Labor in the Old South* (1929), which differs somewhat from the earlier work. C. Vann Woodward wrote an excellent essay on Phillips's work as an introduction to the 1963 paperbound edition of *Life and Labor* (Boston: Little, Brown Company). A fine appraisal of the mythical content of Phillips' work is Richard Hofstadter, "U. B. Phillips and the Plantation Legend," *Journal of Negro History*, XXIX (April, 1944), 109-124. A recent leftist admirer of Phillips is Eugene D. Genovese; see the introduction to his *The Political Economy of Slavery* (New York: Random House, 1965). L. C. Gray recorded his 1911 impressions of Lower South blacks and agriculture in "Southern Agriculture, the Plantation System, and the Negro Problem," *Annals of the American Academy of Political and Social Sciences*, XXXIX (March, 1912), 90-99.

[2]Of Reconstruction and its powerful legends, to about 1920, see (in addition to works cited in previous chapters) James S. Pike, *The Prostrate State: South Carolina under Negro Government* ed. and intro. by Robert F. Durden (New York: Harper and Row, 1968 ed.); Wish, *American Historian*, pp. 209-35; Vernon L.

Wharton, "Reconstruction," in Arthur S. Link and Rembert Patrick, eds., *Writing Southern History: Essays in Honor of Fletcher Melvin Green* (Baton Rouge: Louisiana State University Press, 1965), pp. 295-315; and Bernard A. Weisberger's justly famous essay, "The Dark and Bloody Ground of Reconstruction Historiography," *Journal of Southern History*, XXV (November, 1959), 427-47. Particularly important works on intersectional diplomacy, white "reunification," and popular literature and racism in the North as well as the South are Paul H. Buck, *The Road to Reunion, 1865-1900* (New York: Alfred A. Knopf, 1937); Rayford W. Logan, *The Betrayal of the Negro, 1877-1916* (New York: Collier, 1966 ed.), especially pp. 165-312; and Paul Gaston, *New South Creed*, 17-42. Booker T. Washington set the stage for his Atlanta Exposition appearance and repeated the famous Address in his autobiography, *Up From Slavery* (New York: Doubleday-Page, 1901).

Edgar Gardner Murphy wrote of Reconstruction's continuing burdens in "The Freedman's Progress in the South," *Outlook*, LXVIII (July, 1901), 721-24, especially p. 723. Walter L. Fleming's discussion of the Republican debt question appeared four years later in *Civil War and Reconstruction in Alabama* (New York: Columbia University Press, 1905), especially pp. 571-82. Horance Mann Bond's brilliant reexamination of the problem was presented in "Social and Economic Forces in Alabama Reconstruction," *Journal of Negro History*, XXIII (July, 1938), 290-348.

Quoted remarks about blacks and Reconstruction by Winston and Alderman are from the *Progressive Farmer* (Raleigh), April 23, 1901; and from the draft of Alderman's introduction of Washington (ca. 1901) in the Edwin A. Alderman Papers, University of Virginia Library. On Dixon's novels and Griffith's film, see Woodward, *Origins of the New South*, pp. 352-53; Wharton, "Reconstruction"; and Maxwell Bloomfield, "Dixon's *The Leopard's Spots*: A Study in Popular Racism," *American Quarterly*, XVI (Fall, 1964), 387-401.

William A. Dunning is quoted from his "The Undoing of Reconstruction," *Atlantic Monthly*, LXXXVIII (1901), 437-49. On Hamilton see his manuscript, "The Confession of an Anti-Prohibitionist" (ca. 1905), various scrapbooks, and miscellaneous correspondence in the Joseph Gregoire deRoulhac Hamilton Papers, University of North Carolina Library; also see Steelman, "Progressive Democratic Convention of 1914."

[3]The basic source for the education movement and the Southern Education Board is Louis R. Harlan's superior work, *Separate and Unequal: Public School Campaigns and Racism in the Southern Seaboard States, 1901-1915* (Chapel Hill: University of North Carolina Press, 1958). Harlan's book is based primarily upon the papers of the Board at the University of North Carolina Library, which I also investigated. Also of importance are: Woodward, *Origins of the New South*, pp. 396-406; Dumas Malone, *Edwin A. Alderman, A Biography* (New York: Alfred A. Knopf, 1940), pp. 1-236; Rose Howell Holder, *McIver of North Carolina* (Chapel Hill: University of North Carolina Press,

1957), pp. 1-177; Orr, *Aycock*, pp. 18, 208-09; Clarence Poe, *My First Eighty Years* (Chapel Hill: University of North Carolina Press, 1963), pp. 160-62 (Poe was Aycock's son-in-law and a significant school campaigner himself); and Henry Allen Bullock, *A History of Negro Education in the South, From 1619 to the Present* (Cambridge, Mass.: Harvard University Press, 1967), especially the tables, pp. 177 and 180. An older but still worthy overview is Charles W. Dabney's *Universal Education in the South* (Chapel Hill: University of North Carolina Press, 1936).

Baldwin is quoted by Harlan, *Separate and Unequal*, pp. 77-78. The North Carolina farm editor quoted is Clarence Poe in the *Progressive Farmer*, June 17, 1902. Harvard president Eliot's words were originally quoted by the Boston *Evening Transcript*, February 15, 1907, and were quoted again by Gilbert Stephenson in his *Race Distinctions in American Law*, pp. 163-64.

On Dabney and Coon, see their papers in the University of North Carolina Library; the collections are part of the Southern Education Board group. Edgar Murphy's remarks about the design behind promoting Negro schools is from his "Task of the Leader."

Discussion of Edwin Alderman is based upon materials in the Alderman Papers. See especially: "The Growing South: An Address Delivered before the Civic Forum, in Carnegie Hall, New York City, March 22, 1908," a printed pamphlet; "The Spirit of the South," his address at the University of California commencement, June, 1906; Alderman to Walter H. Page, Mar. 9, 1908; copy of cartoon from *Literary Digest*, XXX (April 22, 1905); "On Teaching History," Alderman's 1886 school institute lecture; "Obligations and Opportunities of Scholarship," a 1900 speech; "The Southern Boy and His Opportunity," his speech at the Jamestown Exposition, 1907; and "Southern Idealism: An Address of Welcome to the American Economic Association and American Historical Association, New Orleans, December 29, 1903," a printed pamphlet.

VI: THE SOUTH, THE WORLD, AND THE QUEST FOR RURAL SEGREGATION

[1] Roland Oliver's biography, *Sir Harry Johnston and the Scramble for Africa* (London: Chatto and Windus, 1957) is a good reference; but much more interesting are Harry H. Johnston, *The Story of My Life* (London: Chatto and Windus, 1923); Johnston's many works, especially *The Negro in the New World* (New York: Macmillan, 1910); Alex Johnston (his brother), *Life and Letters of Sir Harry Johnston* (New York: J. Cape & H. Smith, 1929), in which Alex Johnston had printed much of Sir Harry's correspondence, including quoted items between Johnston and Theodore Roosevelt. See also the two Johnston letters in the Edgar Gardner Murphy Papers; and on Roosevelt and eugenics, see Donald K. Pickens, *Eugenics and Progressivism* (Nashville: Vanderbilt University Press, 1968).

The mid-twentieth century scholarship on slavery which Johnston's *Negro in the New World* anticipated is Frank Tannenbaum, *Slave and Citizen* (New York: Alfred A. Knopf,

1947); and Stanley Elkins, *Slavery: A Problem in American Institutional and Intellectual Life* (Chicago: University of Chicago Press, 1959). The historiographical worm has turned once more, however; recent historians have attacked Tannenbaum and Elkins for the views they shared with Johnston regarding the better conditions of Latin American enslavement.

On American educational and philanthropic work in Africa see Thomas Jesse Jones, *Education in Africa* (New York: Phelps-Stokes Fund, 1922); and Charles T. Loram, "Native Progress and Improvement in Race Relations in South Africa," in *Twenty Year Report of the Phelps-Stokes Fund* (New York: Phelps-Stokes Fund, 1932), pp. 21-92.

[2]On American overseas expansion and racism, particularly with regard to the Philippine Rebellion and the national debate, see Henry F. Graff, ed., *American Imperialism and the Philippine Insurrection* (Boston: Little, Brown and Company, 1969), a useful anthology of differing historians' opinions and original documents; Christopher Lasch, "The Anti-Imperialists, the • Philippines, and the Inequality of Man," *Journal of Southern History*, XXIV (August, 1958), 319-31; James P. Shenton, "Imperialism and Racism," in Donald Sheehan and Harold C. Syrett, eds., *Essays in American Historiography: Papers Presented in Honor of Allan Nevins* (New York: Columbia University Press, 1960), pp. 231-47; Woodward, *Origins of the New South*, 321; Mrs. Jefferson Davis, "Why We Do Not Want the Philippines," *Arena*, XXIII (January, 1900), 1-4.

[3]References utilized and quoted in this section on the Anglo-Boer War and the South African race issue are Nicholas Mansergh, *South Africa, 1906-1961: The Price of Magnaminity* (New York: Frederick A. Praeger, 1962), especially pp. 15-37, 51, 57; L. M. Thompson, *The Unification of South Africa, 1902-1910* (Oxford: Clarendon Press, 1961), especially pp. 11-12. W. K. Hancock, *Smuts: The Fields of Force, 1919-1950* (Cambridge, England: Cambridge University Press, 1968), p. 114; Pierre L. van den Berghe, *South Africa, A Study in Conflict* (Middletown, Conn.: Wesleyan University Press, 1965), especially p. 31; Eric A. Walker, *A History of Southern Africa* (3rd ed.; London: Longmans, 1957), pp. 548-49; William Maynard Swanson, "The Rise of Multiracial Durban: Urban History and Questions of Color in South Africa, 1830-1930," (Harvard Ph.D. dissertation, 1965), Chapter X. See "The Anglo-Boer Struggle," *Arena*, XXIII (March, 1900), for a report on the New York rally. Poe's account of the interview in London with Maurice Evans appeared in *Progressive Farmer*, June 7, 1913.

[4]For examples of the Anglo-American-South African "conversation" on racial policies see A. C. Dicey, "Mr. Bryce On the Relation Between Whites and Blacks," *The Nation*, LXXV (July 10, 1902), 26-28; Murphy, *Problems of the Present South*, 330-35; "An English View of Our Negro Problem," *Harper's Weekly*, XLVIII (April 23, 1904), 612-13 (on Meredith Townsend's book); Alfred Holt Stone, "The Mulatto Factor in the Race Problem," *Atlantic Monthly*, XCI (May,

1903), 658-62; Stone, "The Negro and Agricultural Development," *Annals of the American Academy of Social and Political Science,* XXXV (January, 1910), 8-15. Prof. Matia S. M. Kiwanuka of Makerrere University, Kampala, Uganda, who has extensive research experience in Southern African newspapers and government documents during the period under consideration, testified to the author that white South Africans looked to the American South for segregation laws (interview Oxford, Ohio, April, 1970).

[5]Material on Clarence Poe's early life, career, and philosophy is based upon his thin, chatty autobiography, *My First 80 Years* (Chapel Hill: University of North Carolina Press, 1963); especially pp. 60-105; Steelman's "Progressive Era in N.C." and Gulledge's *North Carolina Conference for Social Service,* pp. 8-33, both of which have references to Poe; and extensive reading of the *Progressive Farmer* under his editorship, 1899-1915.

The Clarence Poe Papers at the North Carolina Department of Archives and History, Raleigh, offered few raw materials, letters on this early period of his adult life when the author consulted them in 1967 and 1968, not long after the Papers were opened to researchers. However, the Papers are a goldmine for copies of his speeches and drafts of his editorials. The following speeches explained and elaborated his vision of "a great rural civilization": "A Great Rural Civilization in North Carolina," speech at Mooresville, North Carolina, July 31, 1913; "What Must We do to Develop a Great Rural Civilization in the Carolinas?" before the Conference for the Common Good, Columbia,

South Carolina, August 6, 1913; "The Organization of Country Communities," n.d. (ca. 1914); "What Must We Do to Develop a Great and Fruitful Civilization in North Carolina," before the North Carolina Conference for Social Service, Feb. 13, 1914; "The Rural Problem and the Rural Community," before the National Conference of Charities and Corrections, Memphis, May 14, 1914; and "The Greater North Carolina—How May It Be Developed," before the Sand Hills Board of Trade, Southern Pines, North Carolina, December 18, 1914. For the transition from rural problems to rural segregation see the *Progressive Farmer,* June 7, June 14, and August 2, 1913.

[6]The section on the rural segregation campaign is based upon: Charles P. Loomis, "The Rise and Decline of the North Carolina Farmers' Union," *North Carolina Historical Review,* VII (July, 1930), 305-25; Loomis, "Activities of the North Carolina Farmers' Union," *ibid.,* (October, 1930), 443-62. The Farmers' Alliance and N.C. State Farmers' Convention also endorsed segregation. (Loomis dispensed with the rural segregation issue in two short sentences.) Steelman, "Progressive Era in N.C.", 630-31, and Steelman, "N. C. Progressive Democratic Convention." And the *Progressive Farmer,* June, 1913— October, 1915, especially August 2, 6, 1913; October 4, 11, 1913; November 8, 1913; and February 13, 20, 27, 1915.

[7]On the defeat of rural segregation see Poe's editorial, *Progressive Farmer,* January 2, 1915, also December 6, 1913. Hugh Bailey notes Booker T. Washington's opposition to the Poe plan in *Liberal-*

ism in the New South, p. 231. See also the *Southern Planter,* (November, 1913), p. 963, for southern white opposition. Westmoreland Davis, the publisher of the *Southern Planter,* was a dairyman and farmer who employed up to thirty-five laborers, many of them black; see Kirby, *Westmoreland Davis,* Chapter II. On the Gilbert Stephenson-Poe exchange and Stephenson's inconsistencies see Stephenson, "The Segregation of the White and Negro Races in Rural Communities of North Carolina," *South Atlantic Quarterly,* XIII (April, 1914), 107-17; Poe, "Rural Land Segregation Between Whites and Negroes: A Reply to Mr. Stephenson," *ibid.,* XIII (July, 1914), 207-12; and Stephenson, *Race Distinctions in American Law,* 356-58 and *passim.* The letter from the Mississippi black appeared in Poe's paper on September 20, 1913. Other letters from Negroes in both Carolinas, Virginia, and Florida appeared in the fall of 1913. W. E. B. DuBois attacked rural segregation in another medium; see *ibid.,* January 30, 1915.

On Poe's criticism of Dixon see *ibid.,* April 15, 1902; and as late as January 4, 1915, Poe referred to lynching as "The Foulest Blot on Southern Civilization." His views on black education and society are most comprehensively stated in his "Message of the White South to the Negro Race," his commencement address (May 26, 1910) at the North Carolina A & M College for the Colored Race, Greensboro; see copy in the Poe Papers.

Poe pursued the miscegenation issue most frequently in the first half of 1914; see especially *Progressive Farmer,* February 21, 1914.

Poe's statistics on the increase of mulattoes since 1870 were compiled by the Rev. A. H. Shannon of Agricultural College, Mississippi. Professor G. W. Paschal of Wake Forest College discredited them in a letter to Poe, *ibid.,* June 13, 1914.

On the end of the segregation campaign see Poe's University of Virginia commencement address ("What Is Justice Between White Man and Black?"), published in two parts, *ibid.,* August 7 and 14, 1915. See also the letters between Poe and Bailey on the issue, dated October 7 and 14, 1915, in the Josiah William Bailey Papers, Duke University Library.

VII: PROGRESSIVE AGRICULTURE

[1]The discussion of urban nostalgia, agrarianism, and the country life movement is based upon Wayne E. Fuller, "The Rural Roots of Progressive Leaders," *Agricultural History,* XLII (January, 1968), 1-13; Levine, *Varieties of Reform Thought,* pp. 17-21 and *passim;* U.S. Congress, Senate, Country Life Commission, *Report of the Country Life Commission,* Document 705, 60th Cong., 2nd Sess. (Washington: Government Printing Office, 1909); Liberty Hyde Bailey, *The Country Life Movement* (New York: Macmillan Company, 1911); Clayton S. Ellsworth, "Theodore Roosevelt's Country Life Commission," *Agricultural History,* XXXIV (October, 1960), 155-72; E. V. Smalley, "Isolation of Life on Prairie Farms," *Atlantic Monthly,* LXXII (September, 1893), 1033-34. Most useful was Betty Carol Clutts's thorough Ohio State University Ph.D. dis-

sertation (1962), "Country Life Aspects of the Progressive Movement."

[2]This and subsequent material on Knapp is based upon Joseph C. Bailey's excellent biography, *Seaman A. Knapp, Schoolmaster of American Agriculture* (New York: Columbia University Press, 1945). See also Alfred C. True, *History of Agricultural Education in the United States, 1785-1925* (Washington: Government Printing Office, 1929).

[3]Sketches of Ragsdale, Lever, Kitchin, Mann, Kolb, Comer, Smith and Parker are based upon the following: "J. Willard Ragsdale . . . Memorial Addresses . . . January 25, 1920," pamphlet in South Caroliniana Library, University of South Carolina; U. S. Congress, House of Representatives, *Biographical Dictionary of the American Congress, 1774-1961* (Washington: Government Printing Office, 1961), 1213-14; J. C. Garlington, comp., *Men of the Time, Sketches of Living Notables* (Spartanburg, S. C.: J. C. Garlington, 1902), p. 256 (on Lever); James C. Hamphill, comp., *Men of Mark in South Carolina,* 5 vols. (Columbia, S.C.: n.p., 1908), III, 274 (on Lever); R. K. Bliss ed., *The Spirit and Philosophy of Extension Work* (New York: n.p., 1952); and Lever's pamphlet-speeches in the South Caroliniana Library. See Claude Kitchin's business records, correspondence and his political papers in the Claude Kitchin Papers, University of North Carolina Library. George Tindall (among others) refers to Kitchin, Ragsdale, Lever and their small-town and rural comrades as "radicals" in *Emergence of the New South,* p. 10. William E. Rhodes, "The Administration of William Hodges Mann, Governor of Virginia, 1910-1914" (University of Virginia master's thesis, 1968); also the William Hodges Mann Papers, University of Virginia Library, especially his business files, the Mann-J. D. Eggleston correspondence, 1913 (on educational reform), and the Mann-Henry D. Flood correspondence, 1912; and the William Hodges Mann Executive Papers, Virginia State Library, Richmond. William W. Rogers, "Reuben F. Kolb: Agricultural Leader of the New South," *Agricultural History,* XXXII (April, 1958), 109-19; and Hackney, *Populism to Progressivism,* pp. 20-21. On Smith see Grantham's exhaustive biography, *Hoke Smith, passim.* On Comer see his business correspondence and farm papers in the Braxton Bragg Comer Papers, University of North Carolina Library. Hugh Bailey quotes McKelway on Comer's mills in *Murphy,* p. 102. On Parker see the general business and the 1910-20 political correspondence, especially: Joseph E. Ransdell to Parker, May 23, 1912, Parker to Robert Roberts, Jr., Apr. 27, 1914, Parker to George Perkins, October 11, 1913 and March 13, 1916 and April 24, 1916. Parker to Albert J. Beveridge, August 6, 1913, Parker to TR, August 21, 1905, Parker to James Beary, January 27, 1914, and C. J. Labarre to Parker, April 20, 1916. Also see T. Harry Williams, *Huey Long, A Biography* (New York: Alfred A. Knopf, 1969), pp. 131-32, 140-45.

[4]This discussion of the relationship between business large and small and scientific farming, and of the eventual recovery of southern agriculture is based upon: Clutts, "Country Life Aspects," pp. 174-76, 183-85, 203; Grant McConnell, *The*

Decline of Agrarian Democracy (Berkeley: University of California Press, 1953), pp. 29-33; W. W. Finley (president of the Southern Railway) to John M. Parker, February 3, 1907, and clippings referring to institute trains in the Lower South in the Parker Papers; *Progressive Farmer*, August 22, 1899 and January 30, 1900 and *passim*, 1899-1914; *Southern Planter*, 1904-1914; Saloutos, *Farmer Movements in the South*, pp. 254-81; Thomas D. Clark, *Three Paths to the Modern South: Education, Agriculture, Conservation* (Baton Rouge: Louisiana State University Press, 1965), pp. 29-95; Thomas D. Clark, *The Emerging South* (New York: Oxford University Press, 1966 ed.), pp. 40-103.

⁵The section concerning T. O. Sandy, Westmoreland Davis, and the Virginia progressive agriculture movement is revised and condensed from Kirby, *Westmoreland Davis*, Chapter II. Main sources of information are the Westmoreland Davis Papers in the University of Virginia Library; the *Southern Planter; Annual Reports* (published by the state at Richmond) of the Virginia Department of Agriculture and Immigration (see especially 1904, 1906, 1910, 1912, 1913, and 1916); and bulletins and programs of the Virginia State Farmers' Institute, copies of which are to be found in the Davis Papers. Additional and special items are: T. O. Sandy, "Farm Demonstration Work," in Virginia State Farmers' Institute, *Proceedings, Ninth Annual Meeting* (Richmond: n.p., 1913), pp. 86-88; William H. Mann, "Virginia's Big Showing," Richmond *Times-Dispatch*, February 6, 1916; and Governor Mann's correspondence with Davis and with "limeburners" in the Mann Executive Papers.

VIII: PROGRESSIVISM IN BLACK

¹For background on the Negro in the late-nineteenth century and on DuBois and William Lewis Bulkley see Logan, *Betrayal of the Negro*; Meier, *Negro Thought in America*; Francis Broderick, *W. E. B. DuBois, Negro Leader in Time of Crisis* (Stanford, Calif.: Stanford University Press, 1959), pp. 1-89; Gilbert Osofsky, *Harlem: The Making of a Ghetto, 1890-1930* (New York: Harper and Row, 1963), pp. 63-65.

²August Meier and Elliott Rudwick, "The Boycott Movement Against Jim Crow Streetcars in the South, 1900-1906," *Journal of American History*, LV (March, 1969), 756-75.

³On black population, population distribution, and black farmers in general see T. Lynn Smith, "The Redistribution of the Negro Population in the United States, 1910-1960," *Journal of Negro History*, LI (July, 1966), 155-73; W. E. B. DuBois and Augustus Granville Dill, eds., *The Negro American Artisan* (Atlanta University Publications, No. 17; 1912), 41-42; W. E. B. DuBois, ed., *The Negro American Family* (Atlanta University Publications, No. 13; 1908), 50-53; Woodward, *Origins of the New South*, pp. 175-204; Saloutos, *Farmer Movements in the South*, pp. 1-68; Baker, *Following the Color Line*, pp. 66-86; Charles H. Otkin, *The Ills of the South* (New York: n.p., 1894); Lewis C. Gray *et al.*, "Farm Ownership and Tenancy," in U.S. Department of Agriculture, *Agricultural Yearbook, 1923* (Washington: Government Printing Office, 1924), p. 513; Benjamin H. Hibbard, "Tenancy in the Southern States," *Quarterly Journal of Economics*, XXVII (May, 1913), 486; and T. Thomas Fortune's eloquent *Black and White: Land, Labor,*

and Politics in the South (1884; New York: Arno Press, 1968 ed.). The basic source for much of this chapter is U.S. Department of Commerce, *Negro Population, 1790-1915* (Washington: Government Printing Office 1918). This monumental document, compiled mainly by segregated black clerks during the Woodrow Wilson administration, contains all decennial census materials plus many charts not to be found in census reports.

[4]On the progress and process of Negro land acquisition see: *Negro Population*, especially the introduction and pp. 557, 571-72; Booker T. Washington, "The Negro As A Farmer," *North American Review*, CXCV (February, 1912), 175-81; Booker T. Washington and W. E. B. DuBois, *The Negro in the South: His Economic Progress in Relation to His Moral and Religious Development* (Philadelphia: G. W. Jacobs, 1907), pp. 105-08; George R. Bentley, *A History of the Freedmen's Bureau* (Philadelphia: University of Pennsylvania Press, 1955), 90-102; Wharton, *Negro in Mississippi*, 58-73; Logan, *Betrayal of the Negro*, 125-46; Baker, *Following the Color Line*, 89-91; W. E. B. DuBois, "The Negro Landholder of Georgia," in U.S. Bureau of Labor *Bulletin* No. 35, Vol. 6 (Washington: Government Printing Office, 1901), pp. 647-777, a source of major import; DuBois, *Souls of Black Folk*, 160-62; Samuel T. Bitting, *Rural Land Ownership Among the Negroes of Virginia, With Special Reference to Albemarle County* (Charlottesville, Va.: Phelps-Stokes Fund, 1915), introduction. The charts are Hibbard's from "Tenancy in the Southern States," p. 488.

[5]The reference to continued landlessness among some rural Negroes and the following material on southern localities and the state of Virginia

are drawn from J. Bradford Laws, "The Negroes of Cinclare Central Factory and Calument Plantation," in U.S. Department of Labor *Bulletin* No. 38, Vol. 7 (Washington, D.C.: Govt. Printing Office, 1902), pp. 95-120; *Negro Population*, p. 554; William Taylor Thom, "The Negroes of Litwalton, Virginia: A Social Study of the 'Oyster Negro'," in U.S. Department of Labor *Bulletin* No. 37, Vol. 6 (Washington: Government Printing Office, 1901), pp. 1115-70; esp. 115-20; Washington and DuBois, *Negro in the South*, pp. 68-70; William Taylor Thom, "The Negroes of Sandy Spring, Maryland, A Social Study," in U.S. Department of Labor *Bulletin* No. 32, Vol. 6 (Washington: Government Printing Office, 1901), pp. 43-102; Bitting, *Rural Land Ownership*, pp. 32, 59-65; *Southern Workman* (Hampton Institute), XXIX (January, 1900), 7-8; *ibid.*, XLI (August, 1912), 470; Charles E. Edgerton, "Progress of Negroes of Virginia as Property Owners," *Science*, XXIII (April 20, 1906), 608.

[6]The following analysis of population growth rates and rural-urban migrations is based upon: *Negro Population*, pp. 26, 112-13; DuBois, "The Negro in the Black Belt," in U.S. Bureau of Labor *Bulletin* No. 22, Vol. 4 (Washington: Government Printing Office, 1899), pp. 401-17. Among other sources, George G. Tindall notes the customary exclusion of blacks from employment in textile mills early in this century in *Emergence of the New South*, pp. 161-65.

[7]The description and analysis of Negro rural self-help, "Bookerism," and the black farming improvement movement is drawn from the following sources listed in order of employment in the text: Washington and DuBois, *Negro in the South*, p.

52; Washington, "The Agricultural Negro," *Arena*, XXVIII (November, 1902), 461-63; R. R. Wright, "The Colored Man and the Small Farm," *Southern Workman*, XXIX (August, 1900), 483; Clutts, "Country Life Aspects," *passim*; Washington, "New Type of Rural School" *Survey*, XXIX (March 15, 1913), 837-38; Washington, "Lease of New Life in Negro Country Homes," *ibid.*, XXII (August, 1909), 616-18; *Southern Workman*, XLI (November, 1912), 623-27; *ibid.*, XLI (April, 1912), 233-34; *ibid.*, XXXVII (April, 1908), 201-02; *ibid.*, XLIII (June, 1914), 335-36; and (February, 1914), 67; Washington, "The Rural Negro Community," *Annals of the American Academy of Political and Social Science*, XXXIX (March, 1912), 81-89; Walter H. Page, "A Journey Through the Southern States, The Changes of Ten Years," *World's Work*, XIV (June, 1907), 9003, 9026-35; Bailey, *Liberalism in the New South*, pp. 78, 119; *Southern Workman*, XXXVII (May, 1908), 262-63; J. W. Church and Carlyle Ellis, "The Devil and Tom Walker, A 'White Folks' Nigger' Who Has Regenerated a Whole County in Tidewater Virginia from Sloth and Crime to Industry and Enlightenment," *World's Work*, XXIV (October, 1912), 698-704; *Southern Workman*, XLI (April, 1912), 233-34; and Thomas Calhoun Walker, *The Honey-Pod Tree, The Life Story of Thomas Calhoun Walker* (New York: John Day Company, 1958); R. L. Smith, "An Uplifting Negro Cooperative Society," *World's Work*, XVI (July, 1908), 10462-66; mention of Smith and the Texas farm organization is also made in Monroe N. Work, comp., *Negro Yearbook, 1918-1919* (Tuskegee, Ala.: Negro Yearbook Publishing Company, 1919), pp. 2-3; see also Meier, *Negro Thought*, pp.

123-34. On agricultural education for blacks see "Farm Training for Negroes," *Survey*, XXXVIII (June 23, 1917), 267-68; True, *History of Agricultural Education*, pp. 284-87; Trustees of the John F. Slater Fund, *Proceedings*, May 11, 1905; October 6, 1905 (New York: Slater Fund, 1905), pp. 11-19, 30-34; W. H. Holtzclaw, *Black Man's Burden* (New York: n.p., 1915), pp. 136-41. Information on the rising impetus of the farmer movement and Negro county agents is found in *Southern Workman*, 1890s, *passim*, and XXXVII (August, 1908), 438-43; *ibid.*, XLI (January, 1912), 6-7; *ibid.*, XLII (April, 1914), 203; *ibid.*, XLIX (March, 1920), 100-01; *ibid.*, XLI (April, 1912), 233; Washington and DuBois, *Negro in the South*, pp. 53-54; *Progressive Farmer*, February 18, 1902; Work, comp. *Negro Yearbook, 1912* (1912), pp. 17-18; and *Negro Yearbook, 1914-1915* (1915), pp. 10-11; James Hardy Dillard *et al.*, *Twenty Year Report of the Phelps-Stokes Fund, 1911-1931* (New York: Phelps-Stokes Fund, 1932), pp. 41-42. Reference to continued black farm acquisition after the onset of the Great Migration is recorded in the *Negro Yearbooks* for *1916-17* (1916), p. 2; and *1922-1923* (1922), p. 5.

EPILOGUE

[1]Headquotes by Clement Eaton and William Styron are from: Eaton, *A History of the Old South* (2nd rev. ed.; New York: Macmillan Company, 1966), p. viii; Styron, "This Quiet Dust," in Willie Morris, ed., *The South Today: 100 Years After Appomattox* (New York: Harper and Row, 1965), p. 17.

On the 1920s (especially on public services and "business progressive" governors) see Tindall's *Emergence of the New South*, Chapters VII and VIII. See also Saloutos, *Farmer Movements in the South*, latter chapters; Clark, *Emerging South*, Chapters I-III; John Hope Franklin, *From Slavery to Freedom: A History of Negro Americans* (3rd ed.; New York: Alfred A. Knopf, 1967), pp. 480-84 on the 1919 riots; Wilbur J. Cash, *The Mind of the South* (New York: Alfred A. Knopf, 1941), pp. 134-41 on the "savage ideal;" Williams, *Huey Long*, Chapters 16-19 on the Long governorship; and David Chalmers, *Hooded Americanism, The History of the Ku Klux Klan* (New York: Doubleday and Company, 1965; 1968 Quadrangle ed.), especially pp. 28-300, Charles C. Alexander, *The Ku Klux Klan in the Southwest* (Lexington: University of Kentucky Press, 1965) on the second KKK; and Kenneth T. Jackson. *The Ku Klux Klan in the City, 1915-1930* (New York: Oxford University Press, 1967).

INDEX